D0854291

RUN FOR YOUR LIFE

Szolda — or Soldier, as his English friend Woolcott calls him — overhears a conversation between two men. They are speaking in Hungarian (which he understands perfectly) and he is convinced the two are planning a murder. Soldier and Woolcott then become dangerously involved trying to prove their story. This is an exciting thriller which has been serialised on television.

RUN FOR YOUR LIFE

LIFE

DAVID LINE

HEINEMANN
NEW WINDMILLS

Heinemann Educational Publishers
Halley Court, Jordan Hill, Oxford OX2 8EJ
a division of Reed Educational & Professional Publishing Ltd
MELBOURNE   AUCKLAND
FLORENCE   PRAGUE   MADRID   ATHENS
SINGAPORE   TOKYO   SAO PAULO
PORTSMOUTH NH   MEXICO CITY
IBADAN   GABORONE   JOHANNESBURG
KAMPALA   NAIROBI

ISBN 0 435 12208 8

First published by Jonathan Cape Ltd 1966
First published in the New Windmill Series 1975
by arrangement with Jonathan Cape Ltd

98 99 2000 19 18 17

Printed in England by Clays Ltd, St Ives plc

This book is for Philip

Chapter One

◆

IT WAS A rainy day in November when I met him first, and about a regiment of them seemed to be bashing him. He was a little dark skinny kid who looked about eight, but I knew he couldn't be because of the school cap. It was our school cap, and we don't take kids under eleven. The cap was in a puddle, and so was this kid. He was down on his knees in it, and that's where they were bashing him.

As far as I could see, he was letting them. He wasn't struggling or yelling or anything. He was just kneeling there sobbing, and doing that pretty quietly.

I said, "All right, break it up."

It was dark in the alley and they had to peer at me.

"Get lost," one of them said, uncertainly.

"Yeah, vanish."

"Scramaroo."

They let go of him all the same.

I could see they were younger than me, and smaller, which was all right except one of them had some kind of cosh in his hand, a piece of hosepipe or something.

"I know you!" this one yelled suddenly, just about the same moment I realized I knew him, too. He was a tough young kid with an elder brother who'd made my life a misery at another school. "You're Woolcott, ain't you? I know where you live, Woolcott. Better shove off if you don't want trouble."

"Yeah, shove."

"Buzz off. He's ours."

I said to the kid, "Get up."

"You leave him alone," the kid with the cosh said. "He started it. He hit one of us."

"Yeah, he was throwing things."

"Were you throwing things?" I said to the kid.

He just shook his head, still sobbing.

"Yes, you did, you rotten little liar! He caught Harris, didn't he, Harris?"

"Right here," Harris said, pointing to his temple. "I've still got a headache."

I said, "What did he throw?"

"He threw a ball. He threw it flipping hard, too. We was in the timber yard and he run away before we could see who done it."

"How do you know it was him, then?"

"He told us," Harris said triumphantly. "He come up and laughed and told us right out, didn't he?"

"Yeah."

"Yeah, right out, he did. He done it last Thursday and he come up just now and said it was him. Laughing, too."

"I only asked for my ball back," the kid said. It was the first time he'd spoken, and I looked at him twice because it was with a foreign accent. "I saw them playing with it and I came up and apologized and asked for it back. It was only an accident. I didn't mean to hit anybody. It went over the wall by mistake."

"Yeah, you rotten little liar, you threw it."

"No, please, I didn't. It's the only ball I've got."

"The only one you *had* ..."

I said, "Give him his ball back."

"You take a jump."

"Give him it back, quick."

They were ganging up round me, and the one with the cosh was fingering it, so I made a quick snatch before he was ready and got it off him.

I said, "Give him his ball."

One of them pulled a ball out of his pocket and dropped it on the ground, and the kid picked it up.

"My brother'll murder you," the kid with the brother said.

"Give him his satchel, too."

"He'll jump about on you. He'll tear you in little pieces. He'll give you such a crunching – "

I said, "If those are your bikes jump on them quick."

Their bikes were leaning up against the alley wall and they got on them and pushed off.

"I wouldn't like to be you," the kid with the brother said.

He said something else, too, but I didn't catch it. They were all laughing as they rode off.

I picked up the kid's cap from the puddle and stuck it on his head.

I said, "You're a bit of a case, aren't you? What do you want to tell them you did it for?"

"They had my ball," the kid said, still sobbing. "I thought they might hit me, but they ought to give it back."

"Give it back! Look, you want to keep away from that lot," I said. "They'd do you up just for fun. Risk a good hiding for a rotten old ball you can buy anywhere for ninepence?"

"I haven't got ninepence," the kid said. "I only get

threepence a week. My mother can't afford any more."

I said, "All right, then, come on," a bit embarrassed, and hoping he'd dry up now.

He didn't dry up. He started telling me his life story.

I said, "Look, you don't have to tell me all this."

"That's all right. I like to tell you."

He said he was Hungarian and his family had had to run away from there. His father had died about a year ago and his mother was having a hard time earning money. He was still going on about it when we got to the end of the street, and I saw with relief – because at least it shut him up – that the gang hadn't gone home yet. They were waiting for us, circling on their bikes. They had lumps of mud.

We got our heads down and ran. The kid still managed to cop a couple down the back of the neck before we got to his gate.

I said, "You'd better tidy up a bit, hadn't you, before you go in?"

"Yes. Thank you."

He was pushing something in my hand, and I thought he wanted me to hold it while he wiped his neck.

He said shyly, "It's a present. I want you to have it."

I looked in my hand and saw three pennies and nearly went up the wall. I said, "Here, I don't want it."

"Please. It's for you."

"I don't want it."

I tried to give it back, but his hand wasn't there and the pennies went rolling in the gutter. He gave a sort of gulp and turned away, and just then I remembered it was all his spending money and he'd given it to me. So I got down and found it.

"Here. Put it in your pocket."

"It's for you."

"Come on." I forced it in his pocket.

"I'm sorry," he said. "I don't know how you do things. I haven't any friends here ... Forgive me."

He looked so weird I said, "All right, forget it. What's your name, anyway?"

"Szolda," he said. "Istvan Szolda."

It sounded like Soldier the way he said it, so I said, "Okay, Soldier – see you again."

His face came whipping round, smiling all over as if I'd given him the best present he could think of.

"Oh, yes, please. Thank you, Woolcott," he said.

I suppose I was hooked from then on.

Chapter Two

◆

HE WAS ELEVEN and he'd been at school two months. His old man had been a university teacher, and he'd got in the school under some special rule, without having to take the exam. He wouldn't have got in any other way because his English was bad, worse than I'm putting it here. He was in the Juniors and he didn't know anybody yet. But he knew me now. He made the most of that.

Because there was always the danger of the gang getting at him again, he started waiting for me to go to school, and again on the way back. I didn't mind. I didn't like him too much. But I didn't mind.

My mother saw him hanging about outside the house one morning.

"Is that boy waiting for you?"

"I suppose so."

"Who is he?"

"I don't know, a Hungarian kid. He hangs around."

"Is he called Szolda?"

"Yeah, something like that."

"Get your nose out of that book at breakfast. And don't say 'yeah'. If you mean yes, say yes."

"Yes," I said, very distinctly.

"Is he a friend of yours?"

"No."

"Try and be friendly to him. They're nice people. You know he's only got a mother, don't you?"

"Yeah. Yes," I said.

"Well, remember she'll be making the same sacrifices for him that I am for you. Why don't you ask him in?"

I got up from the table fast. "I'm going now," I said.

"Have you got a handkerchief?"

"Yeah."

"Not 'yeah' – yes."

The kid was leaning against the gate. He said brightly, "Ready now, Woolcott?"

"*Yeah*," I said, savagely.

He was all right. It was just that he had nothing to say. He didn't know anything about sport, and he didn't have a television. He just agreed with whatever you said. If you told him a joke, even a rotten one, he would laugh himself sick. If you said, "Hold this", or "Fetch that", or "Run there", he would do it. It was like having a dog. My friend Nixon thought I was barmy to go with him. He said, "Why don't you tell him to buzz off? There are plenty of juniors around."

"He doesn't know any."

"That's his problem. We don't want him."

"He's all right," I said.

Nixon used to wait for me at the corner of Handley's Works, and one morning he was going on about last night's television. Every time I laughed and said, "Yeah, wasn't it good?" the kid did the same. After a while this began to annoy Nixon.

"Why don't you shut up?" he said. "I'm not talking to you."

The kid didn't say anything.

"You haven't even got a television," Nixon said.

The kid still didn't say anything. Nixon grew red in the face.

"Are you dumb or something?" he said.

I said, "You just told him to shut up."

"Then why does he laugh like a parrot when I'm talking to you?"

"I don't know," I said.

"Then tell him to shut up. He hasn't even got a television."

"Never mind about that."

"Well, if he hasn't got one, he can shut up about it."

"So can you."

"So can I what?"

"Shut up about it."

"Say that again," Nixon said.

I said it again, and a minute later we were down on the ground. It was the first time we'd had a fight. He got his lip split and I got my trousers torn. He got up and went off.

The kid had been dancing around like a mad flea while this was going on and the minute I got up he started brushing me down.

I said, "Just you leave me alone."

"I'm sorry. I didn't want to cause trouble – "

"And shut up about it!" I said.

It was difficult having him around. Nixon and I made it up, but it was still difficult. Nixon's old man was a doctor and they were going off to Norfolk for Christmas. His grandparents had a farm there. I was supposed to be going with them, but after our fight he didn't mention that any more. I was pretty sure he would mention it if I told the kid to buzz off.

Nixon was like that. If you wanted something you had to be pretty nice to him. If you borrowed his ruler or rode his bike you had to keep on about what a marvellous ruler it was or how it was the best bike in the world. It got a bit sickening after a while. He wasn't always like that. He had a good sense of humour and we had a lot of jokes that nobody else knew about. He was my best friend, really. But I still wouldn't tell the kid to buzz off because of him.

Chapter Three

◆

IT WAS THE beginning of December when the next thing happened and we were rehearsing for the school play. If the rehearsal went on late we had meat pies and stuff at school, and Soldier got hungry and went home by himself. He wasn't in the play.

One morning my mother said, "That little Hungarian boy is outside again. Is he always so pale?"

"Yeah. Yes," I said.

"He seems tired. Does he do a newspaper round?"

"I don't know."

"I'm going to ask him in for a cup of tea."

"I'm going now," I said.

The kid *was* looking a bit queer.

I said to him, "Everything all right, then?"

"Yes."

"No trouble with the gang again?"

"No."

"Okay."

"Woolcott," he said after a couple of minutes. He was gulping as if he had a lump in his throat. "If I tell you something you won't tell anybody?"

"What is it?"

"You won't tell Nixon or anybody?"

"Okay."

"Make a promise."

"All right. Fine. I said so. What is it?"

"Somebody's going to get murdered," he said.

He was looking at me as if I'd said it.

I said, "You what?"

He said, "Honest. It's true."

"Who's going to get murdered?"

"I don't know. I only saw him for a minute."

"How do you know about it?"

"I heard them planning it."

"Heard who planning it?"

"The men who are going to do it."

"What men? What are you talking about?"

He said he'd been to the library the night before. He'd been to pick up a book for his mother. He'd got the book, and then he'd gone over to the reading section to have a look at the motoring magazines. He was keen on that, Soldier. He'd been there a few minutes when a chap near him said, "Right. Here he comes." He'd looked up then, pretty fast, because the chap said it in Hungarian.

Two men were sitting at the other side of the table. He'd noticed them vaguely before. One was looking at his watch and the other at the main door. An old man had come through the main door. He was a cripple with a big boot and a walking-stick. He wore a glove over one hand, evidently to cover an injury, and a pair of thick glasses.

"Every week the same," the man with the watch said in Hungarian. "Ten minutes to seven exactly."

They hadn't spoken after that, and Soldier hadn't read much. At seven o'clock, just as the library was closing, the old man wandered out with a book. The two men got up and wandered after him. Soldier got up and wandered after them.

It's busy in the street outside the library. Buses pull up there and a bloke sells newspapers on the steps. The cripple had a disabled person's three-wheeler parked just past the bus stop, and he got in it and drove off. The two men stood on the library steps and watched him.

"It's too busy here," one of them said in Hungarian.

"I said it was busy," the other replied. "It's always busy here. That's why he does it. I've watched six weeks now."

"All right," the other man said. "Come across. We'll talk about it."

They crossed the road and went into a café. Soldier crossed and went in the café too. There was a pin-table there and a jukebox and a glass case with sandwiches and cakes. The cheapest thing in the case was a slice of cake for threepence, so he paid over all his pocket money and took the slice of cake over to the table where the men were.

The table was near the jukebox and he couldn't hear much of what they said. What he did hear nearly made his hair curl. The men were working out how they could get the cripple some place where they could kill him.

I said, "What do they want to do that for?"

"I don't know," Soldier said. "I'm telling you all I know."

"Go on, then."

It seemed the difficulty was to get the old man in a quiet place. He always went out to busy places. They thought he did it deliberately.

I said, "How do you mean deliberate? Does he know someone is after him?"

"I suppose he must. All I know is he's Hungarian, too.

They said so. And that he's done something wrong, something bad. Wait a minute," he said. "Is there an English word that means – I don't know, to kill *legally* – to pass sentence and kill a person because he's done something bad?"

I couldn't think of any word like that. It seemed a mad sort of word to be discussing on the way to school.

I said, "Look, are you sure you haven't dreamed this – one of your nightmares?"

He'd told me about his nightmares. When they'd run away they had to get over some barbed wire and hide in a ditch, and every now and again he dreamed he had to do it again.

"I didn't dream it," Soldier said. "Look, I haven't slept all night. I don't know what to do."

I said, "It's obvious what to do. Go to the police. What else?" I was getting angry with him rolling his eyes and twitching his face.

"Oh, no," Soldier said. "No, I can't do that. You don't understand."

"Why not?"

"I can't," Soldier said. "They might have a good reason to get him. You don't understand about Hungarians."

I got angrier than ever, him telling me every other word that I didn't understand. We were doing a course called Civics that term at school. I was pretty strong on Civics. I said, "Never mind about I don't understand. We have the rule of law in this country, all right? And when you have it, everybody obeys it, whether he's Chinese, Hungarian or Double Dutch. So you just tell the police and see if they understand."

"*What* do I tell them?" Soldier said. "I only know what I told you. They went out after that. They went out and jumped on a number five bus."

"Let the police sort it out."

"There's not enough to sort out."

"That's up to them."

"No it isn't," he said. "Look, we can't let it happen. We've got to stop it."

"The *police* will."

"But they won't believe me!" Soldier said, practically jumping up and down in a frenzy.

"And nor do I," I said. "Not unless you tell them." And nor I did, angrier than ever then, because I suddenly saw he'd made the whole flaming lot up, just to have something to say, because he never did have anything to say.

"Oh, no, Woolcott," he said in a panic. "Don't *you* say that. *You* mustn't say it. You've *got* to believe it." And he would have said a lot more only we got to Handley's Corner then, and Nixon was there looking none too pleased.

"Come on," he said. "What's the trouble, then? I've been here ages."

He was scowling at Soldier, but Soldier didn't say anything. He didn't say anything the rest of the way. But just at the gates where we went different ways he started tugging my arm. I was chatting with Nixon so I took no notice.

"That word," Soldier said. "That word we were trying to think of."

"What's he on about?" Nixon said.

"I don't know what he's on about."

"That word," Soldier said. "The one that means to kill legally – you know."

"Tell him to buzz off," Nixon said.

"It's 'execute'," Soldier said. "That's what I was trying to think of – 'execute'."

"Buzz off," I said.

Chapter Four

———————◆———————

I DIDN'T FEEL good about it all day. I wasn't bothered about his story. I didn't believe that. It was because I didn't believe it that I felt bad about him. He'd taken the trouble to make it up so he could have something interesting to say, and I'd simply brushed him off.

I kept thinking about him all through maths, and history, and French.

I looked around for him when we came out, but he wasn't there.

I thought about him all the way home, too.

"Your Hungarian friend's a bit late this morning," my mother said, looking out of the window next day.

"He's not my friend."

"Is he ill or something?"

"I don't know what he is."

I looked up and down the street for him, but he wasn't in sight. He wasn't at Handley's Corner, either.

"Hello. So you finally lost him," Nixon said.

"Looks like it."

"Well, good luck."

"Yeah," I said.

They sent a note round in the afternoon saying "Rehearsal Tonight Everyone – This Means You", so after school I went over to the drama room. It was dark in the yard and bike lamps were lit, but I knew he was there even before I saw him. I just felt him, walking beside me.

I said, "Hello, Soldier."

He said, "I'll do what you want now, Woolcott."

"How do you mean?"

"I'll go to the police," he said. "That's what you want, isn't it?"

"Yeah. Okay."

"Will you come with me?"

"If you want."

"I thought I might spot that disabled person's car. I didn't spot it. I've been looking all day," he said.

"Haven't you been at school?"

"No. I've been out walking. I walked nearly eight hours."

I looked at him. He sounded pretty weak and dead-beat.

I said, "Have you eaten anything?"

"I hadn't any money. It doesn't matter," he said. "Let's go to the police now."

"I can't go *now*. I've got a rehearsal."

He said, "Oh," and came to a standstill. I think he thought he only had to come and tell me and I'd be so glad I'd go rushing off with him right away.

I said, "Why don't you go home and get something to eat, and we'll do it in the morning? We'll do it first thing, on the way to school."

He said in a slow weary voice, "No, I couldn't do that. I couldn't leave it overnight. Forget it, then. I'll go myself."

Old Figgis, the master in charge of the rehearsal, had been out in the yard yelling to stragglers to get a move on, but he'd gone in now. I said, "Look – you stay here. I'll go and see if I can get off. I can't promise."

"It doesn't matter," Soldier said.

"I'll see if I can snaffle you something to eat."

"It doesn't matter," Soldier said again, but not very loud.

I went in and found Figgis.

I said, "Can I be excused tonight, sir?"

"No, you can't. Who are you?"

"Woolcott, sir. It's important."

"Nobody excused tonight, Woolcott. What's the trouble?"

"My mother, sir. She's ill."

"Then you ought to have told me earlier."

"I'm sorry, sir. I just heard."

"It's very inconvenient, Woolcott."

"Yes, sir."

"Is it a prescription or something? Is it something another boy could get?"

"No, sir. She's just asking for me, sir."

"Well, damn and blast it, Woolcott," Figgis said.

"Yes, sir. Can I go, sir?"

"It's very inconvenient," Figgis said.

"Yes, sir. Thank you, sir."

I grabbed a pork pie and belted out again.

The kid hadn't moved. I could see his pale face glimmering in the dark.

"Here," I said. "Get stuck into that."

He didn't talk on the way there. He didn't even say thank you. He just wrapped himself round the pork pie and finished it in a couple of minutes. I couldn't tell if he was sulking or just dead-beat. I didn't care much, either. I was getting fed up with him.

We got to the police station and he started walking straight in.

I said, "Just a minute. What are you going to tell them?"

"What I told you. What else do you want me to tell them?"

I said, "Knock off about what *I* want. I don't want anything. Are you sure *you* want to go in there?"

"It won't do any good," he said. "But I'll do it."

"Just run over the story again, then."

He ran over the story again. It sounded wetter than ever. I said, "Listen, are you sure you didn't make this up?"

"I didn't make it up," he said.

"Only things like that don't happen in this country. They might happen somewhere else. You might have read about it and touched it up a bit. I mean – who's going to believe it?"

"Nobody," Soldier said. "I told you that. You don't have to believe it, either."

I thought I'd have one more try. I said, "Soldier – the minute you walk in there it gets serious. It isn't serious just telling me about it. I mean, I'd understand, and we could forget it … Are you sure you wouldn't like to think about it a bit more?"

"No," Soldier said. "I've thought about it enough. I don't want to think about it any more."

"All right," I said. "Let's go in, then."

There were three or four policemen inside, without their helmets. They were doing things at filing cabinets and with ledgers. A sergeant was having a cup of tea at the main desk. He just cocked his eye at us over the cup.

"I want to report a murder," Soldier said.

The sergeant put his cup down rather slowly. He had a moustache behind the cup and it twitched a bit.

"You want to do what?" he said.

"Report a murder."

"Where?"

"I don't know where," Soldier said.

"Who's been murdered?"

"Nobody yet," Soldier said. "That's what I want to tell you."

Nobody said anything while he got it out. The other policemen stopped whatever they were doing and listened, too. The sergeant's moustache twitched a bit about half-way through and he started drinking his tea again. He didn't say anything for quite a while after Soldier had finished, and then he began drumming his fingers thoughtfully on the counter.

He said, "Hm. This chap is a hunchback, is he?"

"Not completely hunched," Soldier said. "Just a bit hunched – because of his boot. His boot and his stick, you see."

"His boot and his stick. And he wore thick glasses and had his hand covered so nobody could see it."

"That's right," Soldier said.

"M'hm. And these other fellows just went out and jumped on a number seven bus."

"Not a number seven," Soldier said. "It was a five. A number five bus."

"A number five?" the sergeant said, opening his eyes

very wide. "I thought you said a seven. I could have sworn you said a seven."

I hadn't been certain of it to begin with because he'd kept his face straight, but I saw now he was laughing at Soldier. I felt my toes curling up.

"You see," the sergeant said, "we've got to be careful about your evidence because it's important. You're important, too, aren't you – I mean, you'd be about the only person for miles who could understand what they were saying, you being a Hungarian, too, eh?"

I said, "He was the only one in that café who could, anyway." I hadn't meant to speak, and I don't know why I did. I suppose it was the sight of Soldier stepping from one aching foot to the other and not even realizing he was being made fun of.

The sergeant gave me about half a minute of his moustache.

"And who might you be?" he said.

"I'm his friend."

"Were you a witness, too?"

"No. I just thought he ought to come and tell you. He's been trying to find the registration number of that invalid car. I thought you'd have some easier way of finding it."

"Did you?" the sergeant said. "Well, how about thinking these brilliant thoughts outside?"

"I've come with him," I said.

"And he'll be coming with you. In about half a minute," the sergeant said. "Outside. In the hall. There's a bench. Go and sit on it."

I went out in the hall and sat on the bench. I could see Soldier through the glass door stepping from one foot to the other. One of the policemen had turned his head to blow his nose, but I could see from the back of his neck he was laughing himself sick. Soldier was out in a couple of minutes.

I said, "What happened?"

"He took my name and address."

"Is that all?"

"That's all," Soldier said.

"Well, what are they going to do about it?"

"I don't know," Soldier said. "I don't care, either. You told me to tell the police and I told them. That's the end of it."

But of course it wasn't.

I woke up in the night and thought about it. I thought about how he'd gone and told the gang he'd thrown the ball even though he knew he'd get a clobbering. I thought about how he'd gone and told the police his story even though he knew they wouldn't believe it. I didn't believe it, either. But I knew suddenly he hadn't made it up. He might have heard it wrong, or got it wrong. But he hadn't made it up.

My mother heard me going downstairs an hour early. She called out, "Where are you going?"

"Out for a bit. I won't be long."

"What about your breakfast?"

"I'll have it later."

"You can't go out without – " she said, but I *was* out then.

I hadn't mentioned anything to him, but I spotted him

right away at the corner of Worple Street. He spotted me at the same time. He just stood there waiting.

I said, "Hi, Soldier."

He said, "Hi," looking at me cautiously.

I said, "You want to do Worple if I do Claremont?"

"All right."

"Work along both sides and I'll see you back this end."

That was how we started covering the district to find the invalid car.

The houses were old and big round there with curving drives. Most had been turned into flats, and there were several cars in each drive.

After a bit I heard him yelling and I came out of a drive and saw him running up the street.

"What is it?"

"Forty-one Worple," he said.

We went round to forty-one Worple. The car was under a plastic cover. It was an invalid car all right. We looked at it for about five minutes.

I said at last, "Well, you got the details?"

"Yes."

"Anything else you need?"

"No."

"Is this the one, then?"

"I don't know," Soldier said.

He said it once more that morning and three times the next.

The third day, I said, "Look, how do we know we've not found the right one yet? They're all alike."

"No they're not," Soldier said. "There are differences,

see. Some have wing mirrors. Some have had bashes. And the tyres are different. You can tell by the tyres."

"Did you see the old man's tyres?"

"No," Soldier said, reluctantly.

"Or whether he had wing mirrors?"

"No."

I said, "What's the point, then? I reckon we'd better turn it in now, don't you?"

"We can't do that," Soldier said. "What else is there if we do? At least we're getting a complete list of all the invalid cars in the district."

"So what?"

"So when we've got it we take it to an office. There must be an office that tells you who the owners are if you give them the numbers. We look down the names and find a Hungarian one."

"How do you know when it is complete? How do you know he even lives round here? He doesn't have to."

"He must live round here. He goes to the library here. They were watching him here."

That didn't mean anything, but I let it go. I said, "Anyway, nobody's going to give that information to a couple of boys."

He didn't say anything, but his face closed up.

I said, "Do you still want to go on with it, then?"

"Yes," he said. "I'm going on with it. You don't have to."

And after a couple of days, I didn't.

Chapter Five

WHAT I'VE WRITTEN here might give the idea I was worrying about Soldier all this time, but actually it wasn't like that. A lot was going on just then. There was the school play for one thing. And I was in trouble with one of the masters for another. Also, there was my mother.

My mother had an afternoon job in a dress shop. She didn't get on too well with the manageress there. She used to tell me every night what she said to the manageress and what the manageress said to her. She didn't bother about losing the job because she could always get another. But it was getting on her nerves; and it got on mine, too.

Also, there was Nixon. Nixon still hadn't said anything about the holiday in Norfolk. We'd made it up, but he hadn't said anything. So that was going on as well.

We had the school play on December the 15th and 16th, and broke up on the 20th. Nixon was going off the 22nd, I knew that. The last day everyone shook hands the way you do, and Nixon came over and shook mine. Suddenly I got in a flaring temper. I didn't let on I was in a temper.

I said, "Have a good holiday, then."

"Yeah," Nixon said, a bit shame-faced. "And you."

"Going to the farm, then?"

"Yeah," Nixon said.

"When are you off?"

"Twenty-second," Nixon said.

"And coming back on the fifth – that was the idea, wasn't it?"

Nixon went red and I thought for a moment he was going to invite me after all, and I hoped he would so I could tell him to go and take a jump. But all he said was, "Yeah, that's it. I hear you're going to Manchester."

"That's right."

"See you next term, then."

"Yeah."

I was still in a temper when I got home. My mother didn't come in till after six. She looked at me a bit carefully, but all she said was, "Did you remember to put the gas on the right number?"

"Yeah."

"And have your tea?"

"Yeah."

I was doing the 'yeahs' deliberately so she would pick on me and we could have a row. I felt like having a row with somebody. She didn't pick on me. She just put her apron on and started seeing to supper.

It wasn't till quite a bit later, after we'd eaten, that she said, "I think we'll take the late-night train to Uncle Will's. That eight o'clock one's always so crowded."

"Okay."

"Don't you think that's a good idea?"

"Yeah. All right. I said so."

She came over and hugged me. "I'm glad you're coming. It wouldn't have been much fun on my own."

I knew it wouldn't be much fun anyway, but I gave her a hug back because all she was saying was she was sorry it had fallen through with Nixon.

We never had to say much to each other. She's pretty shrewd, my mother.

That was the 20th, and we were going away on the 24th, a Saturday night. Why we had to leave it so late was because the dress shop was pretty busy over Christmas and my mother had to work full time till the last minute. It was so busy she fixed up for me to go and work there, too. I had to see to all the wrapping stuff, and there were racks of dresses to fetch in from the vans. Also I made tea in the back room practically all day long. The assistants used to come in and take their shoes off and have a quick cigarette and call me darling. I didn't mind. I got twelve and six a day for it.

I did that for a couple of days, and then on the Friday evening Soldier came round and rang the front door bell. He'd never done that before.

I said, "Hi, Soldier," not too pleased, because we'd just got back.

He said, "Can I talk to you, Woolcott?"

My mother called from the kitchen, "Who is it?"

"A friend of mine."

"Tell him we're eating in five minutes."

"We're eating in five minutes," I said.

"I've been trying to get you all day," Soldier said. "I've been coming round every hour."

"All right, come in then. Just for a minute."

I took him up to my room and switched the light on. His face had the look it had when the business first started. I thought he'd finished his list now and wanted me to go with him to this wonderful office he'd set his heart on. But it wasn't that.

He said, "Woolcott, I've seen them again."

"Where?"

He'd seen them in the library. He'd been going there every evening between six and seven. The two men had turned up, but the old cripple hadn't, and presently the men had gone over to the café again, and Soldier had gone after them.

It seemed the men thought the cripple had been tipped off in some way, and one of them said the whole thing would have to be speeded up now. There was going to be a 'full meeting'. It was to be at 'the school in Amberley Park'.

I said, "What school in Amberley Park? There isn't any school there." Amberley Park was one of the streets I'd covered while looking for the car. I'd been up and down it, both sides. There were ivy-covered houses, a private hotel, British Legion headquarters, the Rotary Club. No schools.

"Yes, there is," Soldier said. "I've been up there. You've got to go right up to the front door to see it. There's a little brass plate there. It's a school of languages."

"And that's where they're meeting?"

"At eleven o'clock tonight."

He was looking at me in a peculiar way.

He said softly, "I went all round it. There's a side entrance without a lock. There's a toilet at the back. The sash is broken and you can get in that way. That's the way I got in."

I said, "You did what?"

"Got in the house," Soldier said. "Through the toilet window. We can go in that way tonight."

I said, "You're barmy!"

"There won't be any *noise*," Soldier said. "Look, I checked that. There isn't even a squeak."

"You're stark raving bonkers!" I was staring at him incredulously. "Look, just you forget it. I'm not breaking in any house, and nor are you. This is for the police."

"*Supper's ready*," my mother called up the stairs.

"I'm not going to the police," Soldier said.

"Yes, you are," I said in an angry whisper – because I'd got him out of the room now and on the landing. "What do you think you can do?"

"We can listen," Soldier said eagerly. "We can get there before they turn up and hear what they plan and *then* go to the police."

"*It's out on the table and getting cold!*" my mother called.

I said, "You get out of here. I'm not going there and nor are you."

"Yes, I am," Soldier said. "I'll wait for you on the corner of Amberley Park, half past ten. You don't have to come if you don't want. But I'll be there."

My mother yelled, "*Are you deaf or something?*" and poked her head round the foot of the stairs and her face changed. "Oh, hello. Aren't you – ?"

"This is Soldier," I said.

"I'm sure the name isn't Soldier," my mother said.

"Szolda," Soldier said. "Istvan Szolda."

"Well, Istvan, come in and have a cup of tea."

"He can't," I said. "He's going now," and I got him to the door.

"Remember what I said," Soldier said. "I'll wait five minutes. I'll still go even if you don't come."

"Good night," I said.

As we were eating, my mother said, "What was it he wanted you to do?"

"Go out with him."

"And are you?"

"No."

"I don't know what's the matter with you. Would it hurt you to go out with him?"

Yeah, I said. But I didn't say it out loud.

I went up to my room at about half past nine and got undressed and into bed and started counting the numbers backwards from a thousand right away, so I would get to sleep quickly.

I didn't get to sleep.

It began to rain after a bit and a drain started guzzling somewhere.

I listened to it for about four hours and then had a look at the clock. It was a quarter past ten. I'd been in bed forty-five minutes. There was still time.

I lay back and licked my lips. Soldier would be getting out just about now. He'd get out and walk through the rain to Amberley Park and wait on the corner there. He'd have a long wait if he was waiting for me.

I turned over and started off on another thousand backwards, and about five minutes later saw it wasn't going to work, and cursed, and turned out and put my jeans on. I put a windcheater on top, and slid my feet into a pair of plimsolls.

I moved softly over to the door, but just then heard my mother coughing in her room and decided against it and went out the other way, through the window and down the drainpipe.

I went across the garden and out through the gate in the fence and nearly had heart failure in the alley when a cat turned towards me with a pair of eyes going like traffic lights.

The street was long and empty, lamp-posts shining on wet pavements. Just for a moment the whole thing seemed so crazy and unreal I half turned to go back. But I knew whatever I did the kid would still go through with it. So I stopped thinking and got my head down and my feet moving. I just hoped he knew what he was doing.

Chapter Six

◆

HE WAS STANDING under a big laurel bush on the corner, and I didn't see him till he moved. His hair was plastered down and his shoulders wet from the dripping bush. He said, "I knew you'd come, Woolcott."

"I only came to tell you – "

He said, "Come on," and walked off.

He'd whispered and I found my own voice dropping as I began telling him all the reasons why I wasn't going into the house. He didn't answer. He just shook his head once or twice. After a couple of minutes, I dried up, too. I don't know what it was. He seemed different.

He slowed momentarily and his eyes went swiftly round.

"What is it?"

"That's the place."

He didn't say anything else. He just walked on. He turned after a few yards and walked back. He didn't stop at the place. He walked right past it again.

I said, "What's it all about, then? What are you doing?"

He said, "All right. Nobody's here. I'll go in now. I'll go in alone. When I whistle, you come, too."

He didn't expect an answer. He went before I opened my mouth.

I hadn't been frightened before. I'd been a bit disturbed and in a temper, but not really frightened. I began to get frightened then. I stood in the calm dripping rain and felt my heart thud.

There was the faintest scrape of gravel and a second or two later a whistle. I went in.

The drive curved round past the front door to a rickety side entrance. Soldier was standing just inside it, waiting. He closed the door behind me and moved off right away, gliding swiftly in the darkness, round to the back of the house. There was a little out-building with the window he'd talked about, and he stopped and fumbled at it.

There was a slight grating sound as it went up. He went in first and held the window for me, and I followed him – and at just the moment he warned me about it felt my foot going into the lavatory bowl. The water didn't come much above my plimsoll, but it set my nerves jangling worse than ever.

He shut the window and we waited there in the cramped toilet, listening to the sounds of the house. He wasn't more than inches from me, but I couldn't see him. Above the creaking and rustling I could hear my heart going *thump*, *thump*, *thump*.

He said softly, "All right, I'll open the door now."

"What's out there?"

"I don't know. We've got a few minutes to find out."

"Look, hang on – "

He'd gone. I went after him. It was dark out there, but not so dark. Light came in from a street lamp through a fanlight. There was a big hall with a round table covered with papers and magazines; a couple of doorways and a flight of stairs.

He wandered off in the dim light by himself, sniffing round like a terrier while I stood petrified by the toilet door, ready to beat it back out of the window. He came back after a minute.

"We'd better try upstairs."

"Look, hadn't we better – ?"

He was gone again. He didn't even look to see if I was following.

I was following.

The broad staircase was carpeted down the centre. There was a half-landing with a little room and another toilet. We rounded the bend to the first landing. Every stair creaked as you trod on it. I felt sick. Soldier's dark shape kept steadily ahead of me.

There were a couple of doors on the landing. Soldier opened them.

"Classrooms."

"Look, Soldier, what do you say if we – "

"There ought to be another room on this floor."

" – wait downstairs?"

He was away again, sniffing down the landing.

"Woolcott." The faintest murmur in the darkness.

I followed it.

There was another door, and he was inside. A sudden thick smell of stale cigar smoke.

He said, "I brought a torch. You can't see it from outside," and a pencil of light came on.

He said, "Shut the door."

I pulled it to behind me.

"Yes. This will be the room."

There were lots of books around, shelves full of books. There was a long mahogany table and leather chairs. There were thick curtains drawn across the windows.

He said, "Do you think we might switch the light on for a second?"

I practically squeaked, "For Pete's sake, no! It will show."

"We've got to find somewhere to hide here."

"Not here, Soldier! Let's wait downstairs. We don't know if they'll come here. When they come in we can see where they go and follow them – "

"No," Soldier said, "that's no good. They'd hear us coming upstairs. Probably they'll leave somebody down below to keep watch."

"Along the landing, then. We don't want to get stuck in here … "

I heard my own voice babbling on. Soldier had already turned away and the finger of light was running along the far wall. I knew in my bones he was right – that this was the room they'd be coming in, and there was something horrible in the idea of being trapped in it, in the stale bitter cigar smoke, with thick curtains at one end, and a door at the other, and nowhere to run if we were spotted, and nobody to hear if we yelled.

He must have had an idea what was in my mind. He said, "Woolcott, if you think it would be a good idea to split up, one up here and one below – "

I said, "I don't know. What do you think?" and hoped he would think yes, so I could make a quick dash down the stairs, out through the toilet window and round the back of the house to the shelter of some welcome dripping bush. And maybe that's what I would have done, except just at that moment a door closed softly below.

There wasn't any possibility of error. It closed softly but

quite firmly, and a second or two later there was a step on the stairs.

His torch had been turned on the wall, but now – I don't know why, shock maybe – it swung suddenly to the ceiling, and as the beam crossed his mouth I saw his lips moving. He seemed to be praying. The beam came down then, quickly, and swung round the room.

There was nowhere to hide. There was nowhere at all to hide. Bookshelves. Mahogany table. Curtains. I saw him going over to the curtains, and in a panic went with him, knowing it was crazy to hide behind curtains because somebody might want to open a window in the stuffy room, and then we'd be cooked, when I saw he wasn't making for the curtains.

There was a little table at the foot of the curtains. There was a china ornament on it, and under the ornament a plush tablecloth that swept to the floor.

He lifted the tablecloth and shone the torch under. There wasn't enough space there. There wasn't enough space for a cat. There were a couple of diagonal bars there to brace the legs. He flashed the torch round the room again, but it was clear there was nowhere else, so we went under the tablecloth, both of us, together.

I don't know how he organized himself. I don't know how I organized myself. I couldn't kneel, or sit, or lean, or rise. I seemed to be crouched over on my fingertips like a sprinter at the ready. And that was the position when the door opened and the light came on.

Chapter Seven

———◆———

THERE WERE TWO of them, and they came in quite briskly and started shifting things about in the room. You get a funny impression of what's going on in a room if you happen to be squashed under a little table in it. The impression I got was that they were throwing all the furniture out, but it was obvious later they were only rearranging it a bit.

One of them came over and opened a window and drew the curtains more tightly, and on his way back managed to jolt the table. Soldier hadn't got his balance yet. He'd tried resting on his elbow, and then on mine, and at the moment was poised with his heel just brushing my fingertips. At the jolt he settled back on the heel.

I tried shaking my hand but he didn't feel it. He just leaned back on me. In some peculiar way he'd got his behind practically in my mouth and the smell of his rain-soaked trousers was half choking me. Beyond biting him there I couldn't see what to do. But he seemed to cotton on presently, and edged himself round, and I felt my fingers again.

More men had come in the room and they'd stopped shifting the furniture now. They were sitting around talking, their voices coming to us with a weird slow-motion booming quality beneath the plush tablecloth.

I saw a chink of light flash in and caught Soldier's fingers raising the edge of the cloth. The air was pretty deadly under there. It had been bad enough to begin with, but

Soldier had turned himself round now, had shambled round in the dark like a turtle so that his forehead was against mine and we were gasping practically into each other's mouths.

I'd lost track of what was going on in the room. There seemed to be about twenty of them there, the voices booming from different points. The door was opening and shutting and people blundering around – the kind of row you hear from another room when you're trying to get to sleep.

I whispered between gasps, "What's happening?"

I could feel his eyelids flickering against my forehead. "They're discussing whether the old man has a gun. They say he has three fingers missing on his right hand."

"How many of them are there?"

"Five men in the room and two downstairs. They're waiting for somebody else."

It made more sense after that and presently I could track the five of them; track the separate voices anyway. One of them seemed to be moving about regularly, going to the door and opening it and walking along the landing and returning and closing the door again. This was what had confused me into thinking there were more of them in the room.

There seemed to be a kind of flutter in the room after a while and I opened my mouth to whisper to Soldier, but he leaned against me sharply and I kept quiet. He was listening, his eyelashes brushing my forehead.

He said in the ghost of a whisper, "The last man's just come. He's walking up the drive now ... " and a silence fell.

I felt Soldier's breath coming quicker against my cheek. The wooden bar under my shin seemed to be cutting it in two, but I couldn't move. A door opened and shut below, and someone began coming up the stairs. He came slowly and he seemed to be carrying something, a load of some kind. He came up a step, and the load came up a step. A pace and a thump. A pace and a thump.

I'd got the idea even before he reached the top, but was dead sure of it as he came along the landing. A pace and a thump. Pace, thump. Soldier gave a sort of gulp and I knew he'd got it, too, and tried to lean against him so he would know I knew, but he whispered it all the same. "It's him, the cripple … "

Pace, thump, pace, thump. Along the landing to the door. And then a pause, a long pause. I had a feeling I was bursting. I had a feeling I had to jump up with the table on my back and yell, "Don't come in! Beat it! They're going to kill you!"

But I didn't jump up and the old man didn't beat it. There was a final shuffle and the door opened, and for a second there was silence, and then a gasp.

I don't know the Hungarian for "No" but I know that's what he said then. "No … No … No … " again and again. He just went on saying it till a voice spoke in the room. It wasn't particularly loud but it shut him up right away. It said, "Bela Stepan Kallai," which I suppose was his name, and then went on in Hungarian.

Some time during the course of it, I felt Soldier trying to move. He'd been gulping a bit and catching his breath, and it occurred to me he was feeling ill or going to faint. I got one hand dangerously up from the floor and caught his wrist, and he shook it back, pretty hard, so I knew he wasn't ill. A bit of row had started up in the room then other voices joining in, so I whispered, "What's the matter?"

"It's not right," Soldier said. "They condemn him without trial! No, it's not right."

"All right."

"It's not right," Soldier said.

He wasn't keeping his voice down particularly. I thought he'd gone mad or something. The hairs at the back of my neck started to rise.

I said, "You stay still."

"It's not right."

I don't know whether he was trying to get up, or if I was restraining him too hard. Whichever it was, he came over against me. He came quite slowly, rolling over on his shoulder, and just as slowly, his weight on me, I rolled away from him, rolled against the table leg, and felt it going, slowly, slowly – the whole operation like one of the boxing films on television when they show you the knock-out for the second time round and the fighter comes floating gently down like a snowflake with his head round sideways as if he's bowing to somebody.

I read somewhere they get the slow-motion effect by running the camera twice as fast to take the picture and slowing it down to show it, and something like this must have happened to my brain the moment the table went over. For it happened, all of it, in the space of seconds, and yet every tiny movement stood out separate and distinct.

There was the ornament going over, just above my head, a dull thump. And immediately after, the other bang

– not much of a bang, a little report like a cap going off, but with a hiss. And my own instant realization that it was a gun, a gun fitted with a silencer – something I'd only read about before.

And then we were up and on our feet, the room blindingly lit after the darkness under the table, and everyone motionless in it like waxworks. They'd swung the table round crosswise so that it was facing the door, and four of them were seated at it, their backs towards us. The old man stood in the doorway with his mouth wide open, staring at the man who had just shot him. It was a little man who had shot him, and the gun looked too big in his hand, a gigantic thing with a barrel about a foot long and a canister stuck on the end of it like a can of Flit – the silencer.

A head turned round from the table, and then others, and I'd got my feet out from under the bars and was running. I think Soldier was there before me, because I remember the man with the gun stepping aside to head him off. There was a weird smile on the man's face. Only his mouth was smiling as if it was twisted that way. And he only took one step, because at that moment the old cripple fell. He never said anything, not a single sound, but his mouth was still wide open and one arm came out as if he meant to make a speech. And the arm fell on the man with the gun, sort of draped round his shoulders so that he slewed round and half fell himself, and as he did so I was at the door, with Soldier there, too, and chairs were tumbling over behind us as the men at the table came bounding after us.

We were on the landing, thumping along it, and I took the first little flight, eight stairs, all in one go, and passed

Soldier; and in the hall below a man came running up from the back somewhere, and saw us, and ran to the foot of the stairs to head us off.

I suppose he'd got up four or five stairs when I saw over the banisters a small side table in the hall below, and without thinking about it, as naturally as if I'd done that kind of thing every day of my life, I'd got myself over the banisters and was jumping. I landed hard on the table and fell over, with the table on me, and a moment later got Soldier in the small of my back and had all the breath knocked out of my body.

But I was up, scrambling to my feet and running, with the man on the stairs tearing back down again, and the entire staircase thundering with feet. And then we were there, in the safety of the toilet, with Soldier locking the door behind us, sobbing for breath, while I opened the window. I let him through first, and just at the last, as I went myself, I slipped again, and got the other foot, the left one, stuck in the lavatory bowl, and wriggled it out, dripping, and snaked through the window.

It was raining still, black out there. Soldier had streaked off, thinking I was following right after him. I thought he must have gone round the front, and that was no good, no good at all, because I remembered suddenly he'd said there were two men below, and we'd only seen one of them in the hall; which meant one would be stationed outside at the front still.

I whistled for him and got no answer, and ran round to the side and saw him there, dimly silhouetted against the glow from the street lamp, waiting for me with the rickety gate open.

The little idiot called out, "Woolcott!" and I hissed back, "Here. Here, you fool!" and after about a lifetime he seemed to cotton on and closed the gate and came running.

There was a wall round the garden, too high to climb. But I'd spotted something in the glow from the street lamp: a concrete bunker, with a big pile of coke up against the wall.

I was still winded from him landing on my back, and seemed scarcely to be breathing. I felt myself running in a kind of daze. It didn't seem to be me running at all. It seemed to be someone else running in the darkness and the rain.

I took the coke at a gallop, and after the coke the bunker, and pausing only to see that he'd made it, too, went over the wall and into the next garden.

We went across three gardens, over sheds and fences, sliding about in the slimy muck of the borders, before it seemed safe to investigate the street again.

There was activity going on farther down outside the house, three or four of them milling around and something being loaded into a van – something floppy and heavy. There was another car there, an invalid three-wheeler, and its lights had been left on. I heard Soldier reading off the number, 42 WPC, and chanting it to himself, so he wouldn't forget, and just about the same moment a church clock struck the quarter, a quarter past eleven. Only an hour since I'd been in bed. I wished with all my heart I was still in it.

I said, "Come on," and we set off in the rain for the police station.

Chapter Eight

◆

IT WAS HALF an hour before we made it, with most of the time spent trembling in bushes. We saw the van come cruising round twice with headlights blazing, evidently looking for us. And a bit later, three men came along on the same job, on foot. We waited, petrified, till they'd gone.

Because I was tired, I'd expected to find everything as before in the police station, the same big moustache drinking the same tea and making the same jokes, and I'd go in there and say, "All right, the joke's over – they finally murdered the man."

But it wasn't like that, because it was nearly midnight now, and a new crew was on: a young sergeant in charge of the desk and a constable sitting reading a paperback book with his feet on the table.

Soldier didn't look up to it, so I started telling it myself, and it must have been convincing because nobody laughed this time. The sergeant suddenly said to the constable, "All right – C.I.D. And get out a call for that car on the radio," and the man stood up and went into the next room. There were voices coming from there, and a big mechanical one like a loudspeaker.

While he was gone, the sergeant turned up the report book and started tapping his pencil against his teeth.

He said, "You were in last week about this."

"That's right, and we got laughed at."

"The man was warned about it."

"What man?"

"This man, owner of car 42 WPC, name of – what is it?" he said, examining the writing more closely. "Kallai? A Mr B. S. Kallai. That the same one?"

I just stared at him.

I said, "How did you find him?"

"Detective branch turned him up the same night through the register of disabled-person vehicles. He said he had no known enemies," the sergeant said, reading, "and was treating the story as a practical joke."

There was a bit too much to take in here. Soldier and I goggled at each other.

"If a charge like that is made," the sergeant said, "it's investigated. Have we got your name and address, by the way?"

"His, not mine."

"Let's have it, then. Do your parents know you're out?"

"No."

"They on the phone?"

I said, "Look, my mother's alone in the house … Can't we leave it for a bit?"

The sergeant grunted, but he took my name and address, and soon after the constable came back from the next room and they talked quietly together. The sergeant lifted the counter flap. "Come in," he said. "We'll be having a brew-up in a minute."

We went in and through to the other room. Two other policemen were in there, one of them on the telephone. The loudspeaker was going, but there was nothing about Amberley Park on it, just reports about stolen and missing cars.

Nothing did come through about Amberley Park for quite a long time, perhaps a quarter of an hour, and then a voice came on the air and said he was speaking from there and it was locked and in darkness and did they want him to break in?

The sergeant said, "They'll be on the blower with that in a minute. Wilson, just check who the owner of the place is. We'll need his permission."

A lot of routine stuff went on then, and I sat and nodded in my chair. I think I told the story again, but can't remember now. It was hot in the room and our clothes were steaming. I could hardly keep my eyes open and my head had started to sing. I had the weirdest feeling I wasn't there at all, that all this was happening to somebody else, and our wires had crossed.

I remember springing bolt upright when the sergeant called my name. He called it quite loudly – I suppose because he'd already called it before. He was grinning at me. He said, "I know somebody who'll find it hard getting up in the morning. Never mind, me lad. You're doing a good job. Try and keep awake a bit longer. We've got a car going to Amberley Park. It's bringing the owner of the premises, and you two had better go with it. The driver will drop you home afterwards. Okay?"

I said okay and a couple of minutes later the car arrived and we went out. The rain had stopped now but it was colder. A policeman was holding open the back door and talking to the passenger inside.

The man made room for us and Soldier got in first and I followed and the door slammed and we were away. Nobody said anything much and it wasn't till we'd been going for a little while that our fellow passenger spoke. He said, "I can't believe anything like this could have happened in my school. Are you absolutely certain of it?" and I felt Soldier begin to tremble against my arm.

I leaned forward to see the man better, and just then we passed a lamp-post and I caught a glimpse of his face, and that was enough. I'd only had a glimpse of it the first time. It had been stiff and shocked then, because we'd just knocked the little table over, and he'd been the first one to turn round and see us. But it wasn't shocked now. It was smiling quite amiably.

"Are you absolutely certain?" he said again.

My mind seemed to stop working. I felt my heart give a single terrific lurch. Soldier began leaning against me, trembling all over, as he tried to push away from the man.

"Are you cold in here?" the man said, leaning forward so that I could see his lips smiling as the lamp-posts flashed past. "You're shivering."

"Shock, sir," one of the policemen said from the front. "Don't bother them too much. We'll need to ask a lot of questions when we get there."

"Of course," the man said, and settled back again.

He was Hungarian; I could tell that from the way he spoke – like Soldier but a lot more correctly.

I said, "Are you – the proprietor of the school?"

"Yes."

And that was all that was said for the rest of the way.

There was a police car outside the house, and the men in

it got out as we drew up. All the police went into a huddle, and then they broke up and two of them came in the house with us.

Soldier was shaking so much I had practically to hold him up, and I wished someone would do the same for me, because just as we went into the hall I remembered it all again.

The upstairs room wasn't smoky now, and it wasn't untidy. They'd shifted the furniture back in place. Even the little table we'd knocked over was upright again with the ornament back on top.

"Is this the room?" one of the policemen said after a moment.

"Yes," I said, looking at the Hungarian.

"Where the man was shot?"

"Yes. Here in the doorway."

They looked at each other and got down and examined the carpet. There was nothing on the carpet.

"Are you sure."

"Of course I'm sure. We were under that little table."

One of the policemen got up and went and examined the table.

He said, "Two of you were under here?"

"It was pretty crowded," I said.

"Yes," he said drily, and came over to us again. He looked at me for several seconds. He said, "Sonny boy, if this is some sort of caper, now would be the time to pack it in – okay?"

"It's the truth – "

"Only when a person is shot close up, it doesn't happen like on the telly, you know."

"I don't know about that – "

"The carpet wouldn't be like it is now."

"He didn't fall on the carpet," I said. "He fell on the man who shot him. He collapsed on him."

"He didn't touch the carpet at all?"

"Not that I saw."

The policemen were looking at each other with a bit more interest; but before they could ask further questions a yell came from downstairs and one went to answer it.

The Hungarian hadn't been doing anything much during this. He'd just sat in a chair and watched us, his lips pursed and shaking his head at the policemen from time to time.

He said softly, "Officer, I think these boys have had a long day. Can't you send them home now?"

"In good time, sir."

"I won't be preferring any charges. But I'll be interested to hear what made them concoct this fantastic story."

"Yes, sir. So shall we."

I was wondering how to get the policeman on one side to tell him about the Hungarian. I couldn't somehow bring myself to tell him while the man was there. But just then the other policeman returned, and the opportunity went. He had a word with his colleague and turned to us.

"All right, boys, you're needed – for an identification."

"An identification. You've found him, then?"

"Yes. We've found him," he said briefly.

I shot a look at the Hungarian as we went out. His lips weren't pursed any more, and he wasn't shaking his head. He was looking thoughtful.

I remember reading once about crooks in America who'd used a hypodermic needle on a boy. The boy knew something about them, and on the way to the police station for questioning, one of the crooks had pricked the boy with this needle. At the station, all the boy's answers had been dopey, because of the needle, and the police thought he was crazy and sent him off. And while he was wandering about in the street, still confused, the crooks had picked him up and bashed his head in. He was called Luigi, this boy. He was thirteen. I remembered about him pretty clearly.

I was remembering a lot more clearly as we went down the stairs. I stuck close to Soldier and hung on to his arm, ready to yell my head off if I felt anything, a needle prick or anything. But there wasn't any need because out in the street they split us up and Soldier and I went on in front. We went in the car that had been waiting outside.

I was so relieved I started telling the driver the moment we started.

I said, "Look, he was one of them!"

"Who was?"

"That Hungarian. The proprietor of the school. He was there when the man was killed."

He swerved a bit when I said it and turned to look at me.

"He's only trying to bluff!" I said. "He's trying to pretend he doesn't know us. He knows us all right. He was the first one to see us, wasn't he, Soldier?"

"The first one," Soldier said.

I said, "Look, you mustn't let him get away!" because he was just driving on, not saying anything, and nor was the man beside him.

"He won't get away," the man said.

"Don't you want to hear about it now?"

"When we get there."

"Where is it we're going?"

"You'll see."

"Is it the mortuary?"

The driver gave a quick grunt. "Not the mortuary," he said.

"Where then?"

"Know Burlington Avenue?"

"Is that where he lived – the cripple?"

"Yes."

"I never did Burlington," Soldier said. He'd improved a lot since leaving the house.

"No. Well. It's hardly in the district."

"I know."

And just then we got to the place.

It wasn't much of a place. It's that stretch of Burlington with little low buildings, a terrace of them, very old, all crumbling and boarded up. They've made a start on clearing them now, but they hadn't then. Anyway, it was one of those. The cripple's car was standing out in the street. We had to come in close to park in front, and I heard Soldier reading off the number, 42 WPC.

A policeman was peering inside it with a torch, but he stopped as we drew up and came over.

He said, "She's been used in the past hour, Bob – the engine's still warm," but our driver shut him up and took him on one side.

It was cold out in the street, a bitter blustering wind that cut through my damp clothes like a knife. I could feel myself shivering inside them like a pea in a pod. I felt as if I'd been kept awake for about three weeks.

The front door of the house was open and a dingy yellow light shone out on to the bit of front garden. Another light was on in an upstairs room, and just as I looked up I saw the silhouette of a policeman staring down at us from the window.

The street seemed to be full of police cars now; there'd been two there when we arrived, and now the one with the Hungarian pulled up in front of us. The policemen had gone into a huddle, and Soldier and I were just standing about. I smelt something on the wind after a moment and looked round and saw it was the Hungarian smoking a cigar. He was standing by himself out in the road. He was standing with his hands in his pockets, his coat collar up and a silk scarf round his neck. He was looking about him rather carefully, first up one end of the street and then the other, and it came to me in a flash he was planning to slip off.

I went over near him right away.

I'd started rugger that term. I'd started the leg tackle. I thought if he moved off in the dark I'd move with him, and if he ran I'd give him the leg tackle. You get weird ideas that time of night. He was a big man, well built, and probably he'd have kicked my head half in. Anyway, I moved near him, and at the same time began whistling a tune so the police would know where I was if anything happened. It was hard to whistle in the wind, and my lips were stiff with fright; and all that happened, he looked round and saw me and began smiling, shaking his head and smiling; and just then the police came out of their huddle and one of them said, "All right. In the house, please," and we went in.

It was a horrible kind of house. It was the kind of house that smells of sweat and vinegar. There was no real floor-covering anywhere, and the stairs rumbled and shook as we went up. I thought they'd be rumbling like that when they carried the cripple down.

Soldier was shivering beside me, and I knew it wasn't the cold now. He whispered, "Woolcott, I don't want to look at him. I couldn't bear to look at him."

I said, "All right, I'll do it," and pressed his arm, none too keen myself.

Voices were coming from a lighted room on the landing and the door was open there. There was a single unshaded bulb dangling on a bit of flex, and it lit up a grim little room. There were two or three chairs and a table, and an iron bed that looked as if it had come off a rubbish heap. There was also a little gas ring in a corner with a pan on it, but just as we got in a policeman stepped back and knocked the pan off. The room seemed to be full of policemen, all too big for it, and trying to find places to put themselves. One of them was seated at a table, and when I saw who else was at the table I felt my knees begin to knock together.

"Right," the policeman at the table said to me. "Is this the man?"

My mouth opened but no words came out.

For it was him. It didn't seem possible for it to be anybody else. He was sitting there, eating a plate of soup, large as life.

"Come in," the cripple said. "I want to talk to you."

Chapter Nine

◆

I SAT DOWN. I had to because I couldn't stand up any longer. I sat down on the bed and Soldier sat down with me. I saw his mouth was open, and realized mine must be, too, and shut it. The only sound in the room was the scrape of boots and the steady shlurping of the cripple at his soup. He kept his eyes on me as he ate, little bright eyes, tiny and sharp like a bird's, peering at me over the thick pebble glasses.

The policeman said, a bit irritably, "Now then, is this the man or isn't it?"

I said, "I think so," unable to take my eyes off him.

"Who you saw shot tonight?"

"Yes."

"And killed."

"I thought he was."

Soldier began to cry then, the steady kind of sobbing I'd heard once before. Nobody took any notice of him.

"All right," the policeman said heavily, and opened a notebook. "Now then, has anyone shot at you tonight, sir?"

"No," the cripple said, shlurping.

"Have you been to forty-seven Amberley Park?"

"Never heard of it," the cripple said.

"Have you been out at all?"

"Why?" the cripple said. "Do I have to get permission to go out in this country?"

I forgot to put he was talking with an accent. He was

talking with an accent even worse than Soldier's. What made it worse was that he was talking with his mouth full. He wasn't a very fancy eater, the cripple. He'd stopped shlurping now and was cleaning out his plate with a piece of bread. He was cramming his mouth with the bread, and when he'd finished he got up and went over to the pan and poured himself out another plate. There wasn't a whole plate of soup left in the pan because the policeman had knocked it over. I remember noting all these details with a kind of wonder – the way he walked, with a pace and a thump, and the light glistening on his tight shiny glove.

I remember noting them because none of them made any sense. I'd seen this man shot. I'd seen him stagger and fall down. I'd seen him bundled in the back of a van. How was it possible for him to be stamping about here getting himself plates of soup? It wasn't possible. But he was doing it. I had the crazy nightmarish feeling that if only I shook my head hard enough I could shake myself right out of this room. I could shake myself back to my own room, to my own bed, with the clock ticking on the mantelpiece and the moonlight white on the wallpaper.

I didn't shake my head. I just sat and stared stupidly and listened to the policeman get on with his interrogation.

The cripple said yes he had been out. He'd been to see an old friend. No, the old friend lived nowhere near Amberley Park.

Was he alone in the house? Yes, he was. His landlady and her daughter had gone off for Christmas. He didn't mind being alone in it. He was looking forward to being even more alone in it when the police went.

He wasn't really bad-tempered about it. He was just
sarcastic. And he smiled a lot so there wasn't anything hard
in the words. It was a strange smile. It was like a dog grinning after some special trick. I remembered the smile long
after I forgot a lot of other things about him.

The questioning took longer than I've put here, and in
the course of it the old man finished his second plate of
soup and his second piece of bread and sat back sucking the
food out of his teeth. He'd been looking at me over the top
of his glasses, and at the end he took them right off and
beckoned to me.

He said, "Come here," and when I did so, "Where have
you seen me before?"

I was going to say *In that place tonight*, but I couldn't say
that. I didn't say anything.

He sat and looked at me, sucking his teeth.

He said suddenly, "A lot of boys laugh at me and throw
stones. You're not one of those boys, are you?"

I licked my lips and said, "No." It didn't sound like my
voice at all.

"I hope not," he said. "That's a bad thing to do. It's a
cruel thing. But I want to tell you – come a bit closer –
what's the matter, you're not frightened of me, are you?"

I said, "No," again, but all the hairs on my neck stood up
suddenly because he touched me with his shiny glove.

He said, "That's right. No need to be frightened of me. I
wouldn't harm you, boy ... You know, there are worse
things than throwing stones. Telling lies is worse than
throwing stones. They make mischief. They cause trouble
for a lot of people. See how many people you've disturbed
tonight with your silly stories. Eh?"

I didn't say anything. He'd been stroking my arm with his glove, but he put it up to my face then. It was hard and cold, the glove. It was like a dog's paw after it's been out in the rain, but smoother than a dog's paw, and harder. I felt knuckles there, but no fingers, and shut my teeth hard so they wouldn't rattle. They rattled all the same. They rattled inside my jaw, and he took the glove away, just about a quarter of an inch, so he could feel my jaw rattling against it.

"Nothing to say now?" he said. "Finished talking, have we, boy? All right, we're friends. You just nod your head and I'll know you'll never tell such silly lies again. Eh?"

So I did nod my head, and he grinned at me again like a clever dog, and took the glove away, and about a couple of minutes later we were all out in the street again.

I've tried hard but I can't remember too well after that. My legs had started to ache. I get these stiff legs. I get them when I've been up too late. It's like toothache, only in the legs. When I was younger I used to cry with it and my mother used to come in and rub my legs with liniment.

Anyway, my legs came on. It was after two in the morning, and I was sick and tired, and I felt the first twinge as we shuffled about waiting for the car. I thought, *Oh, no. Not this, too.* But it was, and just a few minutes after that, in the car, I got it full strength, and started crossing my legs and uncrossing them and hissing to myself and biting my lip.

I remember opening the window because of the cigar smoke – I suppose because the Hungarian had lit up again.

But I can't think now why he was with us. Perhaps the other cars had gone off on patrol. Anyway, he was there.

Soldier's house was first on the way, and we got to it.

He didn't budge.

"What's the matter?" the driver said. "This is your address, isn't it – seventy Wheeler Street?"

"Yes," Soldier said.

"All right. Be at the station at nine in the morning ... What is it now?"

The last question was because Soldier had begun whispering in my ear. I couldn't make out what he was whispering, just *woosh–woosh–woosh*.

I said. "What?" and he said, "Oh come on – come outside," but all strange because his mouth was shaking.

I said, "Outside – why?" and he said, "Because you're staying with me – remember? Come out."

I got out, and the driver turned in his seat, and said, "Where are *you* going now?"

"With me," Soldier said. "He's staying with me."

"Have we got your home address?"

"At the station," Soldier said quickly. "They've got it there."

"All right. Nine o'clock in the morning, the pair of you, okay?"

I said okay and the car drove off and I looked at Soldier and said, "What's all this about?"

"I'm not going home."

"What do you mean?"

"I daren't. They know where I live now. They'll come for me in the night."

I said, "You're crazy!"

"I'm coming with you."

"You're not, you know."

"Yes," Soldier said. "Where else can I go? I don't mind where I sleep. I'll sleep on the floor."

My legs were aching so much I was too sick to argue with him, so I just moved off, not caring whether he came or stayed. He came, of course.

He said, "Woolcott, it's worse than ever now – don't you see?"

"I don't want to talk about it."

"We've got to talk about it."

"Not now we haven't."

"We've got to plan what to – "

"Shut up!" I said. "Just shut up about it!" And he did then, and we completed the journey in silence.

We went up the alley and across the garden and I shinned up the drainpipe, and watched for a few minutes as he tried to do the same. He slipped back on the coalshed so often I thought he'd be doing it all night, so I hissed at him, "Hold it," and went down and let him in the back way. He managed to stumble on the stairs, of course, and my mother, a light sleeper, woke instantly and called, "Who is it?"

I held my breath and said, "Me."

"What's the matter?"

"I've got a stiff leg."

"The liniment's in the bathroom."

"I know. Good night."

"Do you want me to do it for you?"

"No, thanks. Good night."

"All right. Try and sleep."

"Right. Good night."

Try and sleep! If only someone would let me, I thought, and steered the little dope into the bedroom and peeled off half the covers and threw them on the floor for him.

I said, "Here. Use those," and climbed in just as I was, too tired even to take my plimsolls off, and just about half a minute later, it seemed, he was shaking me.

I said, "Wha' – wha'?"

He said, "Woolcott, it wasn't him."

"What wasn't?"

"The cripple. It *wasn't* him."

"All right. Get to sleep."

"You've got to get up now. It's time to get up."

I sat up. There was grey daylight in the room, and it was half past seven. I realized I must have slept over five hours. A moment later I realized something else, too. My mother would be up in a few minutes. I came out of bed fast.

"All right, come on, Soldier. You're getting out of here."

He said, "I know. I'm ready."

He was quite calm. He looked awful, but quite calm. He was sitting on the bed. He'd folded up his blankets and put them back on the bed.

I said, "Didn't you sleep?"

"No. I've been working it out. I've got it worked out now. It wasn't the cripple we saw with the police. It was one of them – one of the men who killed him."

I said, "All right, tell me later."

"No. Now. We haven't got time. We did see him in that house."

"Look, it's finished. It's all over – "

"No, it isn't. It's just started. Listen – just listen and don't say anything. We did see him in that house. We're not crazy. We couldn't both be crazy. We know we saw him – "

"We saw him alive with the police!"

"Not him. It wasn't. It was someone else, dressed up as him."

"Look, we saw him walk. He was crippled!"

"Because of the boot. Anyone could walk like that."

"And his hand."

"A glove. I could wear that glove."

"But – everything about him. The stoop – those thick glasses – his eyes – "

"He couldn't see with the glasses. He kept looking over the top. When he talked to you he took them off – don't you remember?"

I did remember. I remembered pretty well. I remembered his smile, and his eyes, not dim and puckered like the eyes of people who wear strong glasses. Sparkling eyes, lively eyes, smiling up at me like a clever dog.

I said slowly, "But – someone would know what he looked like – someone close to him – "

"Yes. His landlady. His landlady and her daughter. And they've both gone off for the week-end – remember? Probably that's why they picked this week-end so nobody would notice his absence, so nobody would know. But someone does know. We know. Oh, they managed to fool the police. But they know they won't have fooled us, and we might convince somebody else. They know that. So if they still want the week-end to carry out whatever plan they'd worked out, and if they wanted to feel perfectly safe – they'd have to do something about us ... wouldn't they?"

My mouth was dry. I said, "What kind of thing?"

"What do you think?" Soldier said, and nodded as he saw the look in my eyes. "That's why I wouldn't go home last night. Because they knew where I lived."

"You mean you'll have to stay here?"

"No. Not here."

"What then?"

A faint grin came on and off like a weak torch battery.

"You still haven't got it, have you?" he said. "I won't be staying here, and nor will you be. How long do you think it's going to take them to get your address, too? You gave it in at the police station. I stayed awake last night and kept the door open, ready to yell the house down if I heard anything."

Just then we both heard something, and he jumped about a foot.

I said, "It's okay. It's just my mother."

He said, "Oh," and clenched his hands tighter.

"All right, you'd better get moving now. You've got about four minutes before she'll be down. She'll be going to the bathroom. You can have a wash at the kitchen sink, and then wait for me. I'll bring you out some food as soon as I can. You'd better wait out in the alley."

"No, I'm not going out in the alley," he said. "I'm not going out there. I'll wait in the garden. I'll find some place to hide."

I said all right, and he went.

I listened for a bit, but I didn't hear him moving. Soldier

might not have been too good last night, and he mightn't have slept since; but he'd certainly sharpened up again this morning.

Chapter Ten

◆

I DON'T KNOW how I got through breakfast. I sat and watched my mother get through hers. She said, "What's the matter, you're not eating?"

"I'm all right."

"If you don't want the egg, leave it. Take the bacon."

"I don't want it."

"You want another drink?"

"Okay. And toast."

"More toast? I don't know where you're putting it."

I was putting it in my lap. I had my handkerchief there. I'd got three pieces in the handkerchief while she read the paper.

She had another cup of coffee herself and stood up. "I'm just going up to powder my nose. You be ready in two minutes."

I said all right, and waited till I heard her on the stairs, and then shot out the back door.

I couldn't see him in the garden. I looked all round it, and whispered, in a bit of a panic, "Soldier!" And he said, "Here," and I looked up and saw him in the elm tree. It was a bright place to hide. He was brighter than me this morning.

I said, "Here, catch," and threw up the toast tied in my handkerchief and he got it first time and started scoffing right away. I never saw anyone hungrier than that kid. He was always hungry.

I said, "What do you want me to do?"

"When's your mother going out?"

"Now. In just about a minute. I've got to go with her. We go to the shop together."

"Can't you make an excuse and stay behind?"

"No. But I'll come back. I'll think of something and come back."

"No need. I'll meet you out somewhere. I'll meet you in George Square in ten minutes."

"Okay. You can nip up the alley."

"I'm not going in any alley."

"All right. Wait till we've gone and come through the house."

"Won't the back door be locked?"

"I'll see it isn't."

I got back inside just as my mother came down.

"Are you ready now?"

"Yeah."

"Not '*yeah*'. Yes. And look at your jeans. You look as if you slept in them. Why don't you tidy yourself up a bit? Did you put the cat out?"

"Yeah. Yes."

I hadn't put the cat out. It had just run out when I went in the garden.

"All right. I'll lock the back door."

She went and locked it, and I went with her.

"Come on," she called from the hall after a minute. "What are you doing there?"

"Just checking the back door," I said.

We were halfway to the bus stop before I tried the excuse. I said, "Oh, blast it!"

"What is it?"

"I forgot my money."

"What do you want money for?"

"I've got to buy something, lunch-time."

"I'll give you the money," she said, but she smiled as she said it. I hadn't got her Christmas present yet, and she knew I hadn't.

"It's all right. I'll go back."

"Well, if there's something you must buy," she said, still smiling. "Only be quick. We'll be busy today."

I said, "Okay. You carry on. I'll see you there," and got moving.

I looked back after a moment, and she looked back just the same moment, and we smiled and waved at each other, and I was glad of that later, because once or twice during the next few days I didn't think I'd be seeing her again – ever.

Chapter Eleven

———◆———

HE WASN'T IN George Square when I got there. I looked all round and couldn't see him, and then suddenly he darted out of a shop doorway and I realized he'd been watching me from there. He began to get on my wick a bit then. The whole situation did. It had been dangerous enough last night, and dangerous enough when he woke me in the grey early light. But it didn't seem dangerous now. It was broad daylight now. People were walking about in the street, and you didn't have to creep about watching from doorways to see what was happening in it.

I said, "All right, come on, let's get on with it."

He said, "You got any money on you?"

"Yeah." I'd had the money in my pocket all the time. They paid me every day at the shop. The manageress just took twelve and six out of the till and gave me it. I'd been working there three days.

He said, "How much?"

"Thirty-seven and six."

"Can you get any more?"

"Yeah. I get another twelve and six tonight. What do you want money for?"

"You never know," he said.

He was looking pretty horrible. He didn't look too marvellous at the best of times, but this morning he looked horrible. His face looked crumpled and greenish and his eyes were sunk in his head. I could hardly bear to look at him.

We had to cross the square to get to the police station. He said, "Woolcott, I reckon you better do the talking. They laugh at me."

"All right. What do I tell them?"

"That it was the wrong man they saw last night. They've got to send round to him again. They've got to get his boot and his glove off."

I could imagine what they'd say to that.

"All they've got to do is see if he's got three fingers missing from his right hand. They can check that from the cripple's papers. They mark down any kind of physical defect when you come in the country. They did it with me," Soldier said. "The Aliens Office does it."

"You think they're going to bother?"

"No," he said. "I don't think they will. But we've got to try." And suddenly he stiffened, and said, "In here – quick!" I jumped in a shop doorway with him, and smartly, too, because just at that moment I saw for myself.

A man was coming out of the police station. He was coming out briskly and smiling to himself. It was only his mouth that was smiling. I'd seen him doing it the previous night. I'd seen him all in that moment when we came out from under the table and the cripple fell on him. His mouth was smiling because it was twisted that way. He was past us in a few seconds, head down, lip grinning at the pavement.

I said, "Where do you think he's going?"

And Soldier said, "Where do you think? He'll have your address now. Come on," and we went across.

The police station is just a few yards from the main postal sorting office and there's always a lot of vans there and people milling around. Soldier scuttled through so fast, one of the postmen yelled after him. "Watch it – whippet quick!" which was a television joke at the time, and a few of them started larking around trying to catch him, yelling, "What's up – someone pinched your trousers?" (I forgot to put that Soldier always wore very short trousers. I don't know why, but he did, and his spindly bare legs made him look weirder than ever.)

But we got through them and into the police station, and as luck would have it, it was Big Moustache on duty again.

He said, "Ah, the boy detectives!"

I said, "We were told to report here."

"So you were," Big Moustache said, and opened his book and wrote something in it. He did all this very slowly and in a way that set the other policemen grinning and my toes curling inside my shoes. He put his pen down when he'd finished and just looked at us without blinking for about a minute. I tried to look back at him, but couldn't, and presently he said, "You horrible little boys, you! You horrible, miserable little boys. What am I going to do about you?"

He didn't expect us to tell him, but he waited a bit, twitching his moustache.

"I know what I'd like to do with you," he said. "I'd warm the pair of you up so you couldn't sit down for a week. But all I'm *instructed* to do is tell you you've been very naughty and not to do it again ... *So don't!*" he said, bending down over the counter and hanging his moustache about an inch from my nose.

I'd expected this kind of performance, but it was a bit unnerving all the same. I just looked at the counter.

"The owner of the school sent his assistant round here this morning," he said slowly and very precisely. "He is not making any complaint. He is just writing to your parents – so take it to heart, all right?"

I licked my lips. I said, "Did you give him my address?"

"I did," the sergeant said, and waited. "Anything else to say?"

"Yes," Soldier said. I'd heard him panting a bit while he waited for me to speak. "Yes. You've got the wrong man."

He said it in a sort of squeak, and the sergeant looked at him in disbelief. His mouth dropped open.

"You what?" he said softly.

"The cripple. It wasn't him. It was somebody else."

"Who else?"

"I don't know," Soldier said. "But you can check with his papers at the Aliens Office. He should have three fingers missing from his right hand. All you've got to do is get his glove and his boot off and you can see – "

"Hop it!" the sergeant said. His mouth had been working for a bit but nothing had come out. "You hop it – before I go up the wall."

He'd started opening up the counter flap, and I stepped back, but stopped suddenly, ashamed that I'd let Soldier say it instead of me. I said, "Look – just listen for a minute, *please*!"

"Out!" the sergeant said.

"What trouble would it be? It would only take a few minutes, and then you'd see. We *know* it wasn't the cripple. We saw him shot."

"*Get*", said the sergeant, speaking very slowly and in a

choked sort of way, "*out. Both of you. Now. Immediately. Before I go stark staring raving gibbering mad. Hop it. Shoo ...* And let me pretend you're just a nasty dream."

He said the last bit to himself and not to us, because we were out now. He'd shooed us out. He'd come from behind the counter and put a hand behind each of us and shot us through the swing doors. And I found a funny thing had happened to me. I'd got in a flaring temper. I was frightened, but in a temper, too, and I half turned to go back in, but Soldier put his hand on my arm.

"Forget it," he said. "What good can it do?" And we went down the steps and out into the street instead.

We didn't say anything after that. We just started back home. We didn't have to go too far, either. We just had to go to the corner of the street. He was leaning against a lamp-post there, reading a newspaper. A stiff breeze was blowing down the street, and it blew the corner of the newspaper away from his face so we could see his lip grinning into it. It only needed one look and we turned round and went back.

We didn't have anywhere to go in particular. We didn't have anywhere to go at all really. I said, "You got any idea what we ought to do now, Soldier?"

"No," Soldier said.

"We can't go back to the police. We can't go to the shop," I said, ticking off in my mind all the things we couldn't do. "What would be the point of going there? I don't want to get my mother in danger."

"No," Soldier said.

"And nor do you."

"No."

"So what else is there? Have you got any relatives in town – anybody close to you?"

"No."

"Or in the country?"

"No," Soldier said.

I'd got my Uncle Will in Manchester. He knew what I thought about my Uncle Will, so I didn't say anything. He didn't say anything, either, which annoyed me. He seemed to be just waiting for me to ask a question so he could say no.

I said heavily, "All right, if we can't stay here, and we can't go to relations, where are we supposed to go?"

Soldier creased his forehead and thought. "To friends?" he said. "In the country?"

"You got any friends in the country?"

"No."

"Why don't you shut up, then?"

"Have you got any?" Soldier said.

I started to say no, and stopped, because I suddenly remembered I did have one. I had Nixon. Nixon was in the the country.

I said, "Well, there's Nixon."

"That's right," Soldier said.

"What do you mean that's right?"

"That's right he's your friend. He is, isn't he?"

"Yeah."

"That's right, then. That's all I said."

I looked at him but he wasn't looking at me. He wasn't looking at anything in particular.

I said, "Anyway, what could Nixon do?"

"I don't know," Soldier said. "I don't suppose he could do anything by himself."

"What do you mean not by himself?"

"I didn't mean anything," Soldier said.

"You mean Nixon's father?"

"I never even mentioned Nixon's father. I never thought about him."

I suddenly started thinking about him. My toes began to tingle as I thought. I wondered why I'd never thought of him before. He was a pretty good bloke, Nixon's father. He was our doctor. He didn't laugh if you had a pain in your elbow or something. He didn't say run about in school and it will go away. He listened to whatever you told him. Practically everybody in the district went to him. I suddenly remembered Soldier went to him, too, and looked at him suspiciously.

I said, "Nixon's in Norfolk."

"Is he?"

"I told you he was in Norfolk. He's on this farm there with his family. I was going there, too. I told you about it."

"I don't remember," Soldier said. "Whereabouts is it?"

"Near King's Lynn. Just the other side, a village. Called Little Gippings. I told you about that, too."

Nixon had told me and I'd told Soldier. I'd told him it weeks before when I was trying to think of something to say to him.

"How long does it take to get there?" Soldier asked.

"I don't know. Three or four hours, maybe. Anyway," I said, "we haven't got enough for the fare." I said the last bit to trap him, because I was sure now, and he was so eager he fell right in.

"Yes, we have," he said. "We've got thirty-seven and six. It only costs twelve and two, half fare, to get to King's Lynn."

I said, "Oh. How do you know that?" and he gulped a bit but didn't say anything.

I said, "Soldier, you didn't happen to go to the railway station before going to George Square, did you?"

"I did just happen to look in," he said lamely.

He'd worked it out himself. He knew it was no use trying to push me. I had to persuade myself. So he just steered me the way he wanted to go.

He's a tricky little kid, Soldier. He's very tricky. But he's a rotten liar, too, so you can usually get him if you wait. You might have a long wait, though.

Chapter Twelve

◆

THERE WAS A queue about a mile long at the ticket office, so we put off ringing my mother till we knew we'd be getting on the train. I was going to ring her at the shop, and she would tell Soldier's mother. We hadn't worked out what we were going to tell them, but as it happened the point didn't arise because suddenly someone yelled, "The train's going. We'll miss it!" and the queue broke up and people started running.

Soldier and I looked at each other and started running with them.

Nobody stopped us getting on the platform. Nobody could stop us. Two ticket inspectors nearly got knocked over in the rush as the crowd swarmed through the barrier. It was like Christmas on the platform. There were bundles of turkeys and hampers and Christmas trees with their roots in sacking. And it was like Christmas on the train, too, everybody laughing and spluttering after the effort of rushing with luggage. We were jammed in the corridor next to a man in a check coat who was glugging from a whisky bottle. He kept saying "Merry Christmas" and offering everybody drinks from his bottle, and he offered us one, and that got another laugh, and Soldier and I were laughing, too. We couldn't seem to stop laughing. We just hung on to each other and laughed till we ached.

I suppose it was the relief of doing something after all the tension we'd been through. Soldier had improved a lot. The colour had come in his cheeks from running, and soon after the train started his eyes began roaming about and I saw he was working things out again. I started working a few things out myself.

I said, "I tell you what, Soldier. I'll ring my mother from the station at King's Lynn."

"You think so?"

"We'll find a telephone box there."

"All right. Is there anybody else you want to ring?"

"Who else?"

"I don't know," Soldier said.

"You mean Dr Nixon as well? If he picked us up in his car it would save a lot of time."

"Do you know his number?"

"No," I said, dashed.

"Or the name of the people he's staying with?"

"They're staying with Nixon's grandparents."

"Whose parents are they – Nixon's mother's, or his father's?"

"His father's … That's right," I said. "It would be the same name. We could just look it up in the book. How many Nixons can there be with farms at Little Gippings?"

"That's right," Soldier said, and I saw that was another thing he'd already worked out for himself, and I grinned at him, and he grinned back, that busy little brain in top form today.

We didn't say anything after that and just looked out of the window.

It had been slushy in town but there had been no real snow. There was plenty of snow here. The fields were covered with it, and everybody in the corridor was saying what a white Christmas it was going to be. From time to time we'd see a solitary figure walking in the fields, leaving big foot tracks, and the man in the check coat would lean out of the window waving his whisky bottle and yelling Merry Christmas. He'd started to sing a bit now, and people near him were getting fed up and trying to move away. It wasn't easy to move away. The corridor was jammed and people were sitting on their luggage in it. They were sitting on luggage in the carriages, too.

It was a bit better after the first stop, because people got out, and better still after the second because the drunk got out, too. At the last stop before King's Lynn, we even managed to get seats. The train had thinned out a lot, and we got a carriage with only one other person in it.

We'd both of us missed sleep and we dozed off, but woke up again sharply when the train jerked. A few other people had drifted into the carriage, and one of them, a little old lady, was eating sandwiches out of a paper bag. There was ham in some of the sandwiches and egg and tomato in others, and Soldier and I sat and watched hungrily as she got through them.

It was getting on for midday now, and we were pretty peckish. I'd not eaten anything since breakfast. Soldier had eaten my breakfast, up in the elm tree. I sat and felt myself dribbling as I watched the old lady slowly eating sandwiches.

I thought if I smiled at her she might give me one, so I did, and after a bit Soldier noticed and started smiling, too. And the old lady became aware of us after a while, and smiled back, so that for about five minutes the three of us sat nodding at each other like Cheshire cats, until suddenly

I felt Soldier stiffen beside me, and I looked where he was looking and saw there were not just three smilers in the carriage, but four.

A man opposite had had a newspaper in front of his face, but he'd put it down now. He was smiling, too. It only took about half a second to spot there was something wrong with his smile. It didn't get as far as his eyes. Only his lip was smiling, as it always would smile, as we'd seen it smiling once already today.

My stomach began to turn over and over, and just then the train went into a tunnel.

In the blackness, a hand reached out from the other side of the carriage and caught my knee.

I knew it wasn't Soldier's hand because he was sitting beside me. I knew it was an adult's hand because it had wrapped itself round my kneecap. But for a few seconds all I did was shrink in my seat with my flesh crawling and my hair standing up on end. In the darkness I heard something, a paper rustling, and knew instinctively the man was taking out something that he'd got wrapped up – a cosh probably. And I did move then – fast.

I twisted my head sideways, so he would hit the seat-back instead of me, and at the same time drew up my other leg ready to kick out at the slightest movement. And just about at the same moment, I got a whiff of what was in the rustling paper, and brought my leg down again smartly, and managed it just in time, for as the train came out of the tunnel, there we all were, myself sitting up nice and straight, and the old lady leaning over and shaking my knee with one hand and offering me a sandwich from her paper bag with the other.

I said, "No, thanks," because my appetite had suddenly gone, and had to answer no for Soldier, too, because he was beyond speech himself. He was sitting with his mouth wide open staring at the Smiler. The Smiler wasn't staring back at him. He seemed to have gone to sleep. He was sitting with his arms crossed and his eyes shut. But the lip was still smiling.

I said quietly, "Come on," and got up and stepped carefully out of the compartment. Soldier followed me and I let him go first and closed the sliding door behind us, and we went up the corridor very delicately – for some reason on tiptoe (I suppose with some crazy idea not to wake Smiler). And just about ten seconds later I heard the sliding door going again and looked back and realized we needn't have bothered, because Smiler was coming up the corridor, too.

I went practically berserk then. I felt blind and helpless, and my only instinct was to run; so I kicked Soldier on the heel and thumped him hard on the back of the head, and he got the idea and took off up the corridor like a hare.

The train was going a fair lick then. It was going about seventy, rattling and swaying from side to side like a cakewalk. Soldier went swaying from side to side with it, bouncing off the door handles and the window rails like a bullet.

There are two sliding doors between carriages. There's one out to the windy concertina bit over the coupling, and another into the next carriage; so with some idea that it might delay Smiler, I took time off to slam them both shut. It didn't delay him, of course, because as fast as I could shut them, he could open them; and when I looked back at the end of the next carriage he was still there. He wasn't hurrying particularly. There was no need for him to hurry. He knew we weren't going anywhere.

One of the things about a train corridor, there aren't a lot of places to hide in it. The carriages have windows and the corridor is long and straight. Anyone coming up one end doesn't have to rack his brains to work out what happened to the person at the other. But there is another thing. Even the longest corridor, like the longest road, has a turning. There tends, at the end, to be a little bend, and in the little bend a little toilet. And just the moment I thought of it, we got to the end, and there was a toilet, and a man coming out of it and going into the next carriage. And at once, without thought, I grabbed Soldier and yanked him backwards, and a second later we were both in there, and the door bolted, and panting into each other's faces.

It suddenly struck me we seemed to spend half our life hiding in toilets. I heard the sliding door pulling to again, and realized it might be our only hope. The man who had just left the toilet and gone in the next carriage had closed the sliding door behind him. But Smiler wouldn't know who had closed it. He'd seen us run round the bend, and then he'd seen the door close. Wouldn't it seem to him that we had closed it? And that if we'd closed it, we must be in the next carriage? And that if we were there he'd better go, too? And wouldn't our best bet therefore be to wait quietly until he did so, and then nip out and back along the train, and keep moving, and drive him stark staring mad looking for us, and at King's Lynn pop out when he was somewhere else and give him the slip?

Hope began to swell again.

"Woolcott," Soldier said. "What are we going to do?"

"Just keep quiet."

"Shall we pull the emergency cord?"

"Of course not! What for? If we pull the cord the train will stop and the crew will come running along to find out who pulled it. Smiler will find out, too!"

"But how did he find us? He was watching the house."

"He must have kept his eyes on us as well."

The train was bump-bump-bumping along and we were hanging on the little grip, lurching this way and that and yelling in each other's ear. You get a terrific roar of noise in a train toilet. The row comes bouncing back off every wall and even up from the lavatory, too. But I was listening for something else above the noise, and just then I heard it, and gave a brief dance of joy, because it was the sliding door going again.

I said, "Soldier – that was him. We fooled him. He's gone down the train. Just keep perfectly quiet and I'll check."

I gave it a few seconds and unbolted the door cautiously and opened it. There wasn't anybody there. So I waited a few seconds more, even more cautiously, and went right out of the toilet. I went up to the sliding door, and looked through it, and nobody was there, either; and I turned round and grinned, which was about the last time I grinned for a week. Smiler was standing there. He was standing grinning back at me. He was standing about ten yards up the corridor, leaning against a window rail. He wasn't really looking at me but at the window. He could see me reflected there as clearly as I saw him.

I shot back to the toilet then, quicker than I've ever moved in my life, but hadn't quite made it when there was a terrific wham and I was on the floor. I thought in a panic, *He's done it! The little idiot has pulled the emergency cord!* but was wrong because Soldier hadn't pulled the cord. The train had just slammed on its brakes for a sharp reduction of speed and was now chuntering slowly along. I looked round quickly to see if Smiler had come after me, but he hadn't, and as I came up off the floor something else struck me.

There was another door there. There was a door between the toilet door and the sliding door. It was a door out of the train. And from where he was standing, Smiler couldn't see it.

There was no handle on the inside of the door. The handle was on the outside. You had to open the window to get at the handle. It was snowing outside. Calm white fields drifted past as the train chuntered slowly along.

I went slowly back to the toilet, confused and dazed.

I said, "Soldier, can you jump?"

"What do you mean can I jump?"

"Can you jump off the train?"

"What do you mean can I jump off the train?"

His mouth was shaking, and I thought I'd go out of my mind if he kept asking what I meant.

He said, "We can't jump off it. We'd break our necks!"

"No, we wouldn't. It's going quite slow."

It *was* going quite slow. It wasn't going as slow as it had been. And the engine was oof-choof-choofing as if it meant to go a bit quicker soon.

I said, "Come on. We'd better do it now. There isn't much time."

He started saying, "What do you mean?" again, so I put my hand over his mouth and told him as briskly as I could. His mouth was still open as I took my hand away, but he didn't say anything. He just followed me out of the toilet.

I didn't hang about too much. I thought it was best not to think about it, so I just opened the window and got my arm out, and turned the handle and pushed the door open.

I said, "You go first."

"I'm not going first."

I said, "All right," no arguments, and gritted my teeth and went first myself. The idea of him going first was so I could close the door behind me when I went. I knew he wouldn't close the door. He'd just get out on the running board and close his eyes and jump, and the door would go rattling backwards and forwards and Smiler would hear it and come running up to see and jump out after us.

I went out and edged along the running board to leave room for him, so I could still see to the door after he'd got out.

It was cold as charity out there. It was noisy, too, with the wind howling and the train chuffing and picking up speed every second. There wasn't anything much to hold on to, and I just prayed he'd come out quickly. He seemed to take a lifetime, poking one foot out first as if he was testing the water at a pool. I held myself back from dragging him out because I could see he was petrified and moving as fast as he could.

His mouth was open and his eyes, too, wide open and staring. He came out in a series of jerks as if he'd just got a set of new limbs and hadn't run them in yet. He was hanging on the door as if he'd never let go, so I reached over past him and said, "All right, Soldier. Just hang on. I've got to shut the door," and he seemed to understand, and let go, and in the same instant toppled over and fell off.

I didn't look to see what happened to him. I just shut the door and braced myself and jumped, too. The train must have been going about thirty, then, maybe thirty-five – too fast for an easy jump. I felt the wind snatch at me in mid-air, and then my mouth was full of it, full of wind and snow, and I was twisting over in the air and it felt icy and solid. I was rolling then and bumping, the wind so solid I still couldn't say if I'd landed, and then there was a thump and a sharp pain in my knee, and I knew I'd landed, and it all stopped suddenly, and I was sitting there, between railway lines, dizzy, a bit sick, with a pain in my knee. I looked round and saw Soldier sitting between the lines, too, fifty yards away.

The train hooted just then, and I turned to watch it, and was in time to see the back of it disappearing round a bend.

I sat there a bit longer, pulling myself together and waiting for the scenery to get back in place, and then I stood up. Soldier had already started walking towards me.

Just as he got to me, the train hooted once more, distantly, and we looked for it, but couldn't see it this time. There wasn't anything much to see at all: an empty landscape, grey sky, swirling snow, white fields. That was about quarter past twelve on Saturday December 24th. We had just three hours of daylight left.

Chapter Thirteen

◆

ON A LARGE-SCALE map you can get a pretty good idea of Norfolk. It's a big flat bare county, very rural. You get a lot of places there with names like Toodleham and Parsons Charity and Prickwillow. And there are dykes and marshes and fens, plenty of small fens. The railway line runs up between a couple of them, Mare Fen and Burnt Fen, and it was somewhere near there we jumped off.

You can see over on the right there are two main roads, the A.10 and the A.134, both running in the direction of King's Lynn. And there are other roads, too, a whole network of them, very faint and square and regular on the map, like a map of Mars.

This is the sort of country it is, and you can see it all on the map; except that when we jumped off we didn't have one. We had thirty-seven and six and the clothes we stood up in; and after we jumped we had a couple of bruises as well.

Soldier's bruise was on his behind, and he came up holding it, walking a bit funny and with a worried expression on his face. But mine was worse. Mine was the one on my knee, and even if I'd known the trouble it was going to cause, I couldn't have cursed any harder. I just sat down again and cursed for about ten minutes.

Soldier wandered off by himself while I was cursing. He wandered off up the track holding his behind, without saying anything. He didn't say anything when he came back, either. He just stood looking at me.

I said, "Well, what did you see?" And he said, a bit nervously, "Not much, Woolcott. There's not much to see round here."

I said, "There ought to be a road over on the right," and hissed a bit with the pain in my knee. "I saw it when we went through a village a few miles back. It went over there at an angle."

We peered across the fields, but there wasn't anything to see. The snow was coming down too heavily.

I said, "We'd better cut across there and pick up the road and try and get a lift into King's Lynn," and gritted my teeth and stood up. He was too busy holding his behind and looking worried to help me, and as soon as I was up I had to get down again. It was pretty bad, the knee. It made me feel sick just to put any weight on it. I was scared I'd fractured it or something. I sat another five minutes, and then tried again, and it must have gone numb because it wasn't so bad then.

The country is so flat round there they didn't have to dig embankments for the trains. They just laid the track on the ground, and it runs like that for miles. There was a wire fence about ten yards away, and we went over it and into the fields.

The snow was about a foot deep, but the wind had blown it in drifts, and it was up to your armpits in the drifts. We went in a couple of times, and then steered a wide track round, and some time during this Soldier started dropping behind. I heard him yelling and looked round and he was straggling a long way back, so I waited for him. It was pretty ghastly, waiting. I could feel my feet in the snow, icy wet and aching in my plimsolls.

He was moaning when he came up and I said, "What's the matter with you?" but I could see what was the matter. His legs were blue. He didn't have long jeans on. He just had those weird shorts. Above the knee the legs were red where his trousers had whipped them, but below they were bluish-grey.

He said, "Oh, Woolcott – my legs! They're frozen!"

I said, "You want to move a bit faster on them, then," because there wasn't much point softening him up by saying what a good kid he was. We had a long way to go yet. I couldn't even see how far we had to go.

He moaned, "I can't move faster. I keep falling over."

"You want to rest for a bit, then?"

"I don't know," he said, wriggling in the snow. "It's worse standing still."

"Well, what *do* you want?"

He just moved around from one leg to the other, snivelling and waving his hands like a couple of boiled beetroots. All he wanted really was to get his legs out of the snow, but there wasn't any way of doing that. It didn't help to stand about in it, and it wouldn't help to go back. We'd come about a mile. The snow had eased now and I could see the footprints going back farther than I could focus.

I tried rubbing his legs, and that wasn't a success, and I tried carrying him, and nor was that. So I said, "Look, you better hold my hand or something. Maybe that will be easier." And maybe it was, because he stopped snivelling anyway. So we walked on like that, hand in hand like the babes in the wood.

That must have been some time after one. There were only two hours of daylight left then.

The snow came on again about a quarter to two. We knew when it was two because a church clock struck.

Soldier said, "Did you hear that?"

"Yeah."

"What is it?"

"Shut up a minute and listen."

The clock had been sounding the preliminaries, but it started striking then. It struck two.

"*Where* is it?" Soldier said.

I said, "Not far, anyway." You couldn't tell *where* because of the snow. "We must be pretty near the road."

He seemed to take off like a racehorse then. I don't know where he got the energy from.

I said, "Here. Hang on."

"Oh, boy!" Soldier said.

"Slow down, then. We'll get there."

"You think there's a village?"

"There's a church. There ought to be a village."

"With some place to eat in it?"

"Why not?"

"Oh, boy!" Soldier said. "I'm going to have a plate of soup. Then a steak and chips. Then a piece of apple pie. Then – "

I said, "Look, I don't know if – "

"Or spotted dick," Soldier said. "*Instead* of the apple pie. Then – "

I said, "Look, you dry up!" because he was making me nervous. If you want something badly it's best not to talk about it too much. It has a habit of fading away.

"And a banger," Soldier said. "A long brown crinkly banger, with mustard, and fried onions, and – "

"Shut up, you!" I said. "Just shut up, see!"

"Oh, boy!" Soldier said. His lips were wet and he was grinning, but not at me. He was grinning down at the snow, as if it was all waiting for him there, on a big plate with a knife, fork and spoon alongside.

"Oh, boy!" Soldier said. "Oh-boy-oh-boy-oh-boy!"

We got to the road about ten minutes later. We saw the trees first and then the line of little bushes in front of the trees, and scratched our legs going through them, and came out on the road, and looked both ways.

I don't know what we expected to find there. There wasn't anything there. It was just a little country lane with about a foot of snow on it. There wasn't even a footmark in the snow. We stood in silence, our breath hanging in the air, the snow falling dizzily all around.

There was a wood of conifers at the other side of the road gabled with snow. There were telegraph poles, the wires also heaped with snow. It was a nice snow scene, if you like snow scenes. I'd had about enough of snow scenes.

"We did hear the clock, didn't we?" Soldier said pleadingly after a minute.

"Yeah, we heard it," I said, and a moment later noticed he was switching his head round this way and that, listening, as if he ought to hear it ticking or something. He started irritating me all over again. He did these barmy things. He could drive you out of your mind sometimes just watching him. His face had gone weirder, too. It had gone a dirty cement colour. He looked like a garden gnome stuck in the snow.

We waited to see if the clock would strike again, the quarter, but it didn't, so we started off again. There were two ways we could have gone, left or right, but because the train had been going left, we went left, too.

We heard the first sound about ten minutes later. It sounded like somebody calling, and was followed by a sort of crackling like a car backfiring, and soon afterwards by the whine of a car driving off.

"A Ford," Soldier said, listening. "An old V-8. Going fast, too."

It *was* going fast, and I let my breath out with relief. It couldn't go that fast in thick snow. Whatever road it was on, the snow had been cleared off it. So we set off again, a lot more cheerful, and five minutes after that, the clock sounded again, the half hour; only it sounded from behind us, and it sounded a lot farther off.

I didn't say anything. We'd gone wrong, but I didn't say anything. We just kept on. The car had sounded a lot nearer than the clock, so we continued in that direction, trudging with our hands in our pockets. The snow was trickling down my back and behind the ears. I could hear my stomach rumbling as I walked, but I was more irritated than hungry. I felt choked up with irritation. It was getting dark now, and we'd walked three hours. We hadn't seen a living thing, and everything we did was wrong. Soldier didn't say anything, either. I was in a mood to give him a good belting if he did, but he must have known that because he didn't.

Three o'clock struck, faintly.

"Three o'clock," I said.

"Yes," Soldier said.

"It can't be *much* farther now."

"No," Soldier said, still nervous about saying too much.

It wasn't much farther. It was just about two hundred yards. We went round a bend in the road, and there it was, the first light. I was so relieved I felt slightly hysterical.

I said, "Okay, there's your village," but Soldier didn't answer this time at all. He was frowning in the dark, and when he did speak it was apologetically. He said, "Woolcott – it isn't a village."

I could see that myself then. I'd been watching for more lights. There weren't any more lights. There was just this one light. It was coming from a farmhouse. There were a few little buildings round the farmhouse. As we drew nearer a figure came out of one of them, with a torch. A peculiar sort of row came out of the building as he opened and shut the door.

I said, "What's that – a generator?"

"I don't think a generator," Soldier said. "Animals."

I couldn't think what animals made that kind of row. We got a bit closer. The snow had been cleared all round the house. It had been cleared in the little approach road, too. There was banked snow on both sides of the road. Just before the house there was another road, cutting off to the right, evidently the one we'd heard the car go up.

We came out of the deep snow at that point and stamped our feet, and just the same moment the man with the torch turned and started going in the house. So I yelled at him and he swung round quickly. He was an old man and he had to peer at us through the falling snow. He couldn't see too well because he'd switched his torch off now. He suddenly seemed to go mad fumbling with it.

I called, "Hello – we're lost – " and realized in the same moment it wasn't a torch he was fumbling with but something bigger and longer, and a moment later was down on my knees and a noise like a bomb was going off just above the spot where I'd been standing.

He'd fired at us. The old maniac had fired a shotgun.

I saw with incredulity that Soldier was on the ground, too, flat on his face, and for one crazy moment thought he'd been hit. But he hadn't been hit. He'd just dropped there with fright.

The old man had started yelling when he fired. I couldn't make out all he was yelling, just, "Get out of it, you thieving rogues! Go on, get out of it … !"

I called, "Look – you've made a mistake! We're lost," and came up off my knees to show him we were only boys so he wouldn't reload. But he was already reloading, clicking and bashing about with the gun in such a businesslike way, I got down again, fast, and made it just in time as a second load of shot blasted out.

Soldier didn't wait to see how quick he could reload again. I felt a sharp kick and looked round and saw him scuttling away, on hands and knees, like a big awkward rabbit, and I slithered round and went after him. At the deep snow, we got up and ran. We ran as fast as we could, which wasn't very fast, but the old man didn't bother firing again. He just stood there, silhouetted against the light, with his shotgun raised.

I yelled, "You crazy old nit!"

"He's mad!" Soldier said.

"Nutty as a fruit cake!"

"What's he want to fire for?"

I said, "You know what – he was doing it before. That was firing we heard, not a car backfiring. He was firing at the car."

"So that's why it took off so fast," Soldier said. "What's he firing *for*?"

We stood there, panting and trembling, watching him. He couldn't see us against the dark background of trees, but he knew we were there. He wandered about in the yard for a bit, looking towards us and listening.

It got very cold as we stood and watched him. The snow petered out but an icy wind sprang up. I could hear Soldier's teeth chattering.

After a few minutes the old chap gave a sort of snort and turned and went into the house; but he left the door open – I suppose so he could come out again fast if he heard anything.

"What do we do now?" Soldier said. He was trembling in the wind like a jelly.

I was so full of rage and misery I couldn't think. I knew we couldn't hang about in the wind and the snow. I knew suddenly I had to get my feet out of the snow. I just couldn't bear them in there any longer. There wasn't any snow in the farmyard ... The light was streaming across it all the way to the little approach road. The light fell short of where we were standing by about fifty yards. If anyone was watching from the window to see if we crossed it ...

I couldn't bear explaining the **risk** to him. I just said, "Come on," and moved off, and heard his teeth chattering steadily behind me as he followed.

There was a window each side of the front door, and I kept my eyes on them, scared to death one would suddenly open and a load of shot come blasting out. Nothing like that happened. We slipped through the light and into the shadow by the snowbanks. I had a terrible urge to stamp my feet there, to stamp the snow off, but I resisted it and tiptoed past, making for the shelter of the outbuildings.

The peculiar animal sound grew louder as we approached. It wasn't a lowing or a snuffling or a grunting. It was a – what? A *chrob-robbling*. *Chrobble-grobble-chrob-grob* ...

Turkeys! Why hadn't I realized turkeys? Norfolk turkeys. I suddenly realized something else. The old man had been guarding them with his shotgun. He'd been guarding them from spivs trying to thieve them – to flog for Christmas in the big cities. It was Christmas Eve tonight. It didn't seem too much like Christmas Eve.

An open barn stood next to the turkey house. I stopped in the opening and listened, trying to make out if any other livestock were in there. There didn't seem to be. I went cautiously in, feeling my way in pitch blackness.

There was straw on the floor, and a number of big objects lying around. I couldn't make out what they were. An oil drum? An old water tank?

There didn't seem to be anything to sit on, so I sat on the floor, and gasped with the pleasure of it, and heard in the darkness another gasp, and knew Soldier had just sat on it, too; and I lay back full length and let my limbs come back to life.

I could hear Soldier's stomach rumbling, and realized my own was doing the same. I was realizing quite a few things just then; that my knee was aching and I was wet through, and absolutely sick with weariness and hunger, when there was suddenly a rustling in the straw, and Soldier came up off it, flapping like a great bat; and a moment later I was up myself, a rat clinging to my jeans. I'd put my hand down and felt it there, the whole length of it, whiskers and tail, and had thrown it off, and it had run back and bitten me.

I don't know what happened then. I was kicking out with my feet, and Soldier was blundering against me. He was still flapping about (the rat stuck in his jersey, wriggling and squeaking there) but he never let out a sound; just danced about in complete silence; and either he fell against me, or I tripped him, but whichever it was, he went stumbling and skittering the full length of the barn, and fetched up heavily against something and tins started falling.

If you've ever been in a supermarket and reached out for a can of tomato soup and found the whole stack tumbling, you get an idea what it was like then, only it was worse, because whatever Soldier had landed against was metal and hollow and the tins came bouncing off it like thunder; and all in the space of seconds the turkeys next door seemed to go mad.

I never heard a turkey scream before. About two hundred of them started screaming then, all together. We stood in the dark, petrified, till I heard something else, a single enraged yell and the sound of boots running, and without thinking about it, found I was running, too, towards the entrance.

Soldier had the same idea and we came rocketing together in a kind of lunatic embrace, and tangled, and went over in the doorway, still locked together like Siamese twins; which was just as well because the same moment the old nut-case decided to loose off at us. He loosed off with his gun about a yard above where we were, just about where we would have been, and blew a hole through the back of his barn, and seemed to go crazier than his turkeys.

He yelled, "All right, you asked for it, now you'll get it! I'll murder you! I'll cripple you! Stay still while I get you!"

We didn't bother taking him up on the offer. We scrambled up and hared past him across the yard to the approach road and had got there before he could loose off again. He was out of luck this time, too, because we were running well then. I never even noticed my knee while I was running.

We stopped when we got to the side road. I'd been thinking about it while we ran. There was no point going back the way we'd come. I thought if the car had gone up the side road we ought to go up it, too, because at least there'd be car tracks to walk in instead of deep snow. I couldn't face walking in snow any more.

Soldier seemed to have the same idea, and we turned in there without a word. There was a powdering of snow over the car tracks, but you could feel the tyre marks frozen underneath. We slowed down to a walk then, and right away my knee came on. It felt as if someone was twisting it with a screwdriver. It made me sick, the pain, but I didn't say anything. We just kept on walking again. Four o'clock struck as we walked.

Chapter Fourteen

———— ♦ ————

BY FIVE WE were still hobbling up the road. I'd given up hope now. All I was interested in was staying on my feet. Soldier had started making funny blubbery noises, and had fallen over once or twice. Just as the sky started clearing he fell over again.

I waited around like a patient cart-horse for him to pick himself up. He didn't pick himself up. This time he just sat there making blubbering sounds.

I said, "All right, what's the matter?"

"I can't walk any more," Soldier said.

"What do you want to do – swim?"

"I can't walk," Soldier said.

I said, "Look – you want your steak, don't you? That steak and chips?"

I don't know if it was the steak and chips or just his behind freezing up on the ice, but he broke out snivelling then. I let him snivel for a bit, and cursed softly to myself. I could hardly stand on the bad leg. I stood on the other, and gathered up strength, and bent down and biffed him. He was so surprised he came up off the ice like a squirrel.

I said, "When you want another, just sit down again," and pushed him and he stumbled and was walking again.

He needed a couple more biffs as the moon came out, because he could see where we were then, and he practically gave up. He just started throwing himself about.

I said, "Listen, I haven't the strength to keep bashing you. Just make up your mind what you want to do."

"I want to go back," he said, snivelling.

"Back where?"

"To that house. To try and speak to the man. There isn't anything here."

There wasn't a lot. There seemed to be trackless wastes either side of the road. There'd been a little wood on the right when we started but that had petered out now. There wasn't even a bush in sight. The wind blew fine and free for miles. It had even started chilling the backs of my eyeballs.

I couldn't bear arguing any more, and I didn't plan to leave him there, so I just bent wearily to biff him again; and stopped halfway. I thought I was seeing things. There was a house there. There was a house about half a mile away, out in the snow, the moon just catching the corner as I bent.

I didn't dare take my eyes off it. I said, "Soldier, look at that," still bending so I wouldn't lose it. And he came up slowly on his knees and followed my arm and said, "It's a – isn't it a house?"

I didn't answer him. I just set off towards it. I waded right out in the deep snow, and cut diagonally across, keeping it in sight all the time.

There was nothing round the house. There was no wall or fence or anything. It was just stuck there, by itself, out in the snow. It was a little house. It didn't seem to get any bigger as we drew nearer; then we got very near, and I saw why.

It wasn't a house. It was a hut, a low stone hut, about ten feet square. An iron chimney pipe stuck out of the top. No smoke came out of the chimney and no light came out of the hut.

My spirits didn't sink exactly. They didn't have room to sink. But I saw there'd be no food for us here, or warmth, and that if we wanted to get in we'd probably have to break in. I thought we probably would. We'd walked five hours now. We couldn't walk any more.

There was a barred window but no door. I walked round looking for the door, and found it the other side. It was a ramshackle door. It didn't look as if it would need much of a shove to break it in, but I tried the handle first. The door opened right away. I went in.

There was a sweaty sort of smell inside. There was a wooden floor, a table, a cupboard, camp bed; everything neat and tidy. There was also an iron stove with a box of matches on it, and above it a storm lamp hanging on a nail. I reached up and got the lamp down and shook it and found there was oil in. I struck a match and lifted the glass and lit it. Soldier gave a sort of sigh as the lamp came on, and flaked out on the bed.

There was a big flat sack on the bed, a kind of eiderdown, stuffed with sheep's wool. It didn't look too clean and bits of wool had dropped out of it. The sweaty smell was coming from the wool. It suddenly struck me it was a shepherd's hut. I held the lamp and looked round it.

There was a bundle of firewood and a pile of old newspapers behind the stove, and a torn sack with a bit of coal in it. So we could have a fire.

There was an open tin of condensed milk in the cupboard, and a packet of sugar and one of tea. So we could have a cup of tea as well, if we had a cup. There didn't seem to be a cup. There was a spoon and fork and a pack of cards. There was a pile of old football coupons and a pair of cracked spectacles. There was a last year's calendar and a box with a lot of old gubbins in it like boot laces and buttons. There wasn't any cup.

In a numb sort of way I set about looking for a cup, till it suddenly struck me he'd need something to boil his tea in as well as to drink it out of, and I lifted the lamp and looked round for a shelf, and found one, up in the shadows of the opposite wall, and a whole new treasure trove as well.

There was a cup. There was a billy can for water, and a plate. There were two tins of baked beans and a bottle of sauce, and a piece of paper with a cheese sandwich in it. It was a pretty old sandwich, but my head swam as I smelt it. Food!

Soldier seemed to have passed out on the bed. I said, "Soldier, are you all right?"

He said, "Yeah."

He didn't look all right, but at least he looked comfortable.

I said, "We've got food here. Wake up."

But even the magic word didn't rouse him. I thought I'd better leave him to it.

I went outside and filled the billy with snow, and made the fire and waited for it to come up. It came up pretty quickly. I sat and watched it, the top of my head lifting off with dizziness and fatigue.

When the stove was hot enough, I took the lid off and set the billy there, and about ten minutes later it started bubbling. I put two spoons of tea in, and stirred it till it looked the right colour, and poured Soldier out the first cup, and added condensed milk and sugar.

I said, "Here you are, cup of tea."

He sat up slowly. He could hardly hold the cup, so I held it. It was pretty hot, and he just sipped. He looked better after a few sips. I drank the rest of the cup, and poured out another, and we shared that, too. I felt a marvellous sort of glow starting up with the second cup. I lay on the sack and felt waves of heat coming out of the stove, and looked about in the lamplight and my head went round and round.

It was like Aladdin's cave after what we'd been through. I could imagine the shepherd spending a night there, the stove roaring, the lamp lit; poring over his football coupons through his cracked spectacles. Even the smell of the sheep's wool wasn't too bad when you got used to it. It seemed to add something to the special fug in there.

I lay on the sack and took in the fug and planned the night's programme. First of all, a meal. A can of beans and half a sandwich each. Another cup of tea. A wash. Make up the fire. Sleep.

Soldier got up and started prowling while I made up the programme. His private radar took him right to the beans, and I saw him standing there in the lamplight having a good time just looking at the picture on the label. The picture showed a pile of beans steaming under a great mound of tomato sauce, and I let him enjoy it for a bit till I got up and started work.

I threw out the tea and filled up with fresh snow, and set it to boil, and punched the top of the can with a fork and put it in the water. Then we sat and watched it heat up. I watched till I couldn't stand the marvellous smell coming out the top any more, and then I got up and laid the table.

There wasn't a lot to lay. There was just the plate, spoon and fork. The shepherd must have used his own knife. I threw out the cheese, which had gone green, and put the two slices of bread on the plate, and the sauce bottle next to it. Then I washed the cup out with snow, and that was the lot.

Soldier hadn't moved during this. He just stood over the beans, swooning with the smell. But he turned then, in a sort of trance, and started making movements with his hands.

"You got the thing, then, Woolcott?"

"What thing?"

"The thing for the can. To get the beans out. The what-do-you-call-it."

The tin-opener.

I looked in the cupboard and on the shelf and behind the stove. I looked under the bed and on top of the cupboard and round the back of it. I had every button and bootlace out of the box. There wasn't a tin-opener. There wasn't anything that would do for a tin-opener.

We didn't have any beans that night. I bent the fork and spoon trying to get them, and then Soldier tried and bent them all the other way, but he didn't get them, either. All we got was a dribble of sauce out of the tins. So we mixed it with what was in the bottle and put it in the hot water and broke the bread in, and had soup instead. Afterwards we had another cup of tea and went to bed.

It was light in the hut when I came to, bright light, snow light. There was a sharp scraping and thumping going on somewhere, and Soldier wasn't there. I got up and went to the door, and saw him out there, working in the snow.

He'd found a stone. He was working on the baked-bean tins with the stone. He was muttering at them, too busy to see me, and I shivered a bit and blinked in the blinding white light.

It was cold and hard everywhere. There was the sharp choking smell of freezing air, and I breathed in and took a good lungful of it. It was quite calm now, no wind, all dazzle and glitter as far as the eye could see. Our footprints of the night before went round the hut like a dotted line. I could hear something faintly – bells. I remembered then.

I said, "Soldier," and he looked up.

I said, "Soldier, do you know what day it is?"

"What day?"

"Christmas Day, Soldier."

He said, "Oh," and looked from me to the can in his hand, and then back at me.

"Merry Christmas," Soldier said.

"Yeah," I said, and went back in.

Chapter Fifteen

◆

THERE WASN'T ANYTHING for breakfast except tea, so we had two cups of tea, and washed up, and left three bob in the cupboard for the food and fuel we'd taken, and set off. My knee wasn't bending this morning. It didn't hurt till I tried to bend it, and then hurt so much I could hardly move for a few minutes. After that I kept it stiff. It slowed us down a lot.

We saw the bus from a long way off. It was flat as a pancake for miles around. The road we were on was just a track across a fen. There was a bit of other traffic on the main road apart from the bus. We counted six cars as we trudged to the bus stop. They looked like fly specks, moving very slowly across the horizon. They weren't really moving slowly. They were well out of sight when we finally got to the stop. A printed schedule was stuck up on the post, and we examined it, breathing heavily.

There were only three buses on Christmas Day. There was one at eight, one at ten and one at two thirty. It looked as if we'd just missed the middle one.

I stood and rested my leg and looked around. The road was a slushy chocolate-coloured mess in a great blanket of white. Nothing was moving on it now. It was utterly silent.

We didn't say anything to each other. We just leaned one each side of the bus stop and started waiting, for a lift.

We waited half an hour, and then got moving again.

Three cars had gone by, but they hadn't stopped. I'd tried yelling special Christmas greetings after the last one with the idea the language might annoy the driver so much he'd stop and sort us out. Maybe he didn't hear.

Anyway, some time after half past ten we were on the move again.

About a mile up the road there was a row of what looked like farmworkers' cottages, and as we came level a man who was picking brussels sprouts in the front straightened up and looked at us.

I said, "Good morning."

He didn't say anything. He just stared. His eyes were crossed.

I said, "Is there a phone round here? We're stuck."

He picked up his basket and turned round and went into the house. We waited a moment, and then he slammed the bolt.

"Maybe he's deaf, or dumb," Soldier said.

"Maybe he's the village idiot, too."

"Let's try next door."

"Forget it. None of them has a phone here." You could see they hadn't. The telephone lines went past the row of houses. "There's bound to be one, though, with all these people. There'll be a public one somewhere near. Let's carry on."

We carried on. Ten minutes later we saw one.

My hands were so cold I could hardly turn the pages of the directory, but I found it at last: "Nixon, Ralph, Top-cross Farm, Little Gippings."

"Just a minute," Soldier said as I picked up the phone. "How are you going to tell him where we are?"

"Give him this number. He can find out from that, can't he?"

"I don't know," Soldier said. "We ought to have asked at the cottages."

"All right, we ought, but we didn't."

"Ask the operator, then."

I dialled and waited. As I waited I thought about it.

"Ask her what?" I said.

"Where we are."

"Number, please," the operator said.

"Where are we?" I said.

"Pardon?"

I got a bit flustered. I said, "I'm sorry, we're lost. Can you tell me where I'm speaking from?"

I gave her the number, and she said hold on, and I did. It was smelly in the box, and cold. There was even ice on the inside. It seemed to take a long time to find out.

"Hello, caller," the operator said.

"Hello."

"You're at Donnybanks, near Wittle."

"Where's that?"

"Wittle is four miles from King's Lynn."

"And how far am I from Wittle?"

"Oh, a couple of miles."

"I see."

"Is that all?"

"No. I want a number."

I gave her the number and waited again. I waited a long time again.

"Hello, caller."

"Hello."

"Your Little Gippings number isn't answering."

"*Isn't answering?*"

Something in my voice made hers a bit more human.

"Maybe they're at church," she said.

I hadn't thought of that. I said, "Oh."

"Why don't you try again in half an hour or so?"

"All right. Thanks."

"Merry Christmas."

"Merry Christmas."

There wasn't any point in hanging about there for half an hour, so we set off to walk to this Wittle. I didn't even try to get a lift this time. Soldier made a few half-hearted attempts, but I didn't. I thought if there was a taxi at Wittle, I'd get it, whatever it cost. What could it cost, anyway? It couldn't cost more than thirty-four and six. I'd got thirty-four and six left.

The road was very slushy now and I couldn't get on in it. There were puddles of water and bits of ice flung up by the cars. I went skidding about, wrenching my leg and biting my lip. We seemed hardly to be moving at all.

I said after a bit, "How far do you think we've gone now?"

"Not far," Soldier said glumly. "Not half a mile. It must have gone half an hour easily."

"All right, keep your eyes open for another phone box."

There wasn't another phone box, but there was a house presently. The house was on the telephone. You could see the wires running down to it. It was quite a way off, up a track on the left. It seemed to be a farmhouse. There were buildings round it.

We stood and looked at it for a bit.

I said, "What do you reckon?"

"I don't know," Soldier said.

"We could ask to use the phone and pay for it."

"Maybe we could pay for some food, too," Soldier said.

"Come on, then."

A car had been up and down the track and there were a lot of footmarks. The house sat in a great ocean of white. Smoke was coming from a chimney.

There was a big drive running from the front to the back door. I didn't know which door we ought to try, but suddenly the front one opened, and a man was standing there. He was wearing a cardigan and carpet slippers, and he was smoking a pipe. He didn't come out in the snow with his slippers. He just waited for us to come to him.

I said, "Merry Christmas," and smiled.

He said, "Merry Christmas," but didn't smile back.

"We're stuck. I wonder if we could use your phone?"

"Come in."

We went in, and my legs went suddenly weak. It was like a great fragrant oven in there. Something wonderful was cooking in the kitchen and there was the scent of burning logs. There were paper and tinsel decorations in the hall, and a lot of noise going on, a radio playing somewhere, and a couple of kids running about upstairs.

A woman came out of the kitchen just as we went in, an elderly woman about the same age as the man. She had a pinny on, and there was sweat on her forehead and on her lip, just the same as my granny used to have when she cooked.

"Couple of boys lost themselves," the man said. "They want to use the phone."

"We'd pay for it," Soldier said quickly.

"*Pay* for it?" the woman said.

"And for any food you can let us have. We're starving. Merry Christmas," Soldier said.

You've got to hand it to Soldier. He's the craftiest little kid I ever met.

The woman said warmly, "Merry Christmas! Merry Christmas both of you! Pay for your food on Christmas Day? And just look at you – you're absolutely perished. Come in the kitchen."

"Just a minute," the man said. "Let them phone first," and he led us across the hall.

One of the kids had run halfway down the stairs while this was going on, and was stuck over the banisters watching us. He was a kid of about four, and they'd been dressing up, up there, because all he had on was a bowler hat and nothing else. A younger woman ran down and scooped him up and he kept yelling, "Who is it? What's he want?" as she ran back upstairs with him.

There was a phone on a table by the foot of the stairs, but the man led us past that. "In here," he said, and opened a door.

Soldier and I went in and looked round the little room, and then at each other. There wasn't a phone. I turned to the man to tell him so, but he wasn't there any more. He was at the other side of the door, and it was just closing. I heard the bolt go just as I got to it. He'd locked us in.

I said, "Here, what's happening?" and started rattling the door, but while I was rattling it I heard him talking, not a yard away, and stopped so I could hear what he was saying. He was talking on the phone. He was getting a number, and yelling for the radio to be turned down, and then the woman had run in from the kitchen, and the kids were running downstairs, and it was bedlam out there. He'd got his number then, and he was talking, and it suddenly hit me what it was all about.

He was saying, "That's right, the boys that escaped from Borstal. One of them talking a bit foreign, as you said ... Yes. Half an hour. Fine."

I yelled, "We're not from Borstal! We haven't escaped from anywhere!" But he never even heard, because a terrific row had started then. The older woman was screaming she wouldn't have it, locking young boys up on Christmas Day. And he was yelling back we weren't just ordinary boys, we were young criminals, and we'd catch our death of cold or starvation or have to commit more crimes if the authorities didn't pick us up, and it was for our own good really. And then the kids were pleading to have a look at us, and the man cleared them all out, and there was silence.

Soldier and I looked at each other and then round the room. It was perfectly bare. There was a stone floor and a little barred window high up on one wall, much too high to reach without a step-ladder. There wasn't even a table or chair.

Soldier sat on the floor and put his head between his knees.

He said faintly, "So they've found us, the gang."

"Yeah."

"And now we've really had it."

"Have we?" I said.

Chapter Sixteen

◆

THERE'D BEEN SOMETHING familiar about the room
when we first came in, but I didn't know what it was. I did
now. It must have been the woman reminding me of my
granny. My granny'd had a room like this. She'd lived out
in the country, too. She'd had a room *just* like it. It was a
pantry, and there was a little cupboard off it where she used
to keep jam and pickles. One time I was barmy for her
pickled walnuts and she wouldn't let me have any more,
and I got in from the garden through a window and took
them. It was a window in the cupboard.

I wondered if this room had a cupboard, and went hunt-
ing round the walls, and found it; found the spot where it
had been, anyway, because it was nailed up and painted
over now.

There was just one nail. It had been hammered in and
bent over to keep the door tight shut. It had been hammered in so hard the head was stuck deep in the wood. It
was a pretty hopeless job without a knife, but I had a go at
it. I tried a sixpence, and rubbed the paint off the nail head,
and then tried with a penny and a half a crown. My fingers
were sore and one was bleeding, but I got the nail head up
a bit. I got it up enough to twist it round from the door, so
that all we had to do was pull the door open, except there
was nothing to pull. There was just a little screw hole,
painted over, where the knob had once been. Everything
was painted over, including the crack between the door

and the door-frame. There was nowhere you could get your hand in to give a tug.

Soldier had got up while I was doing this. He'd stood behind, watching me, and he said suddenly, "Just a minute," and I looked round and saw he was on the floor. He'd got his hand under the door. There was a little gap there, too narrow to get my hand in, but he pulled it out enough so I could, and I squatted down, and got a good grip, and gave a sudden terrific yank.

The door went *ershloomsh*, and the paint started ripping all the way up. Just the same moment I heard something else, footsteps, and let the door go, and we were both on our feet, with our backs to it, when the room door opened and the man and woman came in.

She'd brought us cups of tea, and he'd brought us a couple of mince pies each. She tried to smile at us, but he just looked away. He was pretty embarrassed. He said, "I'm sorry, boys. I wouldn't have done it, except the police – It'll be better for you – " And then they went. We just stood there with the tea and plates, looking at each other. We waited till the footsteps had gone, and then put the stuff on the floor and got back to the cupboard.

We were inside it in about ten seconds.

It was just as I remembered, narrow shelves all round, and a little window that slid up. There was dust and cob-webs round the window catch, but I clambered up on the shelves and cleared the muck, and the window opened first go. I stuck my head out.

We were at the back of the house. There was a yard, very tidy and cleared of snow, and a range of farm buildings beyond. The buildings went off to the right, past the house.

There was a drop of about six feet from where I was look-ing. I didn't know how I was going to manage with my knee, but there was no point hanging around, so I said, "Okay, Soldier, let's go."

He said, "Hold on," and I looked round and saw he was back in the room, cramming mince pies in his pockets. "Okay," he said.

"I'm going out feet first, backwards. You do the same and I'll catch you."

He said okay again and I turned and went out the way I'd told him. I got my legs out the window and sat on the sill and twisted round so I was looking back in the cup-board, and hung on the sill with my hands, and then dropped. I knew it was going to hurt, b‍ ‍ the jolt in my knee nearly made me sick. I was still trying not to be sick when I got his plimsoll in my ear, and I turned and caught him as he dropped.

We started off to the right, away from the house. The cleared stretch didn't last long and we came to deep snow. There were a whole lot of footprints going round the house to the drive. and just a single set of big ones, made by gumboots, going there and back to an old barn. We didn't want to go to the barn, but beyond it I could see telegraph poles – the main road – so we went that way, too, planting our feet in the gumboot prints, so our own wouldn't show. We'd got about fifty yards when Soldier said, "Listen!"

"What is it?"

It was a car, evidently turning in the drive and labouring in the snow. The house was in the way so we couldn't see it. We could hear it pretty well.

"An old Ford," Soldier said. "V-8. Same one we heard yesterday."

He was terrific at cars, Soldier. You could always go by what he said.

We got over to the barn, fast. There was nothing else for it. It was obvious we weren't going to have time to get to the road. They'd go in the room and find the cupboard open and come out looking for us. Our only hope was that they might follow the wrong tracks.

It was a wooden barn, with an open doorway like the one at the turkey farm, but with a loft on top. There was straw on the floor, and a few household throw-outs like bottomless chairs and old toys. You got up to the loft by a ladder, but someone had shoved it up there. You could just see the edge sticking out of the trapdoor. A man with a walking stick could probably hook the ladder down easily enough. We didn't have a walking stick.

The car had stopped now, and we could hear voices.

I said desperately, "Here, get on my back, see if you can reach the ladder."

He got up, but he couldn't.

"How far short are you?"

"Couple of feet."

"Stand on my shoulders."

"I can't."

"Try!"

He tried. He nearly kicked my ear off, but I kept my mouth shut. Something had started up in the house now. I thought they'd got in the room and found the cupboard open. They'd be out any minute now.

He'd got his heel in my collar bone and was grinding it

as he tried to lift himself. I didn't think I'd be able to bear it. I nearly bit my lip through.

"I – I can't!" he said, and all of a sudden I *couldn't* bear it, and wriggled my shoulder, and he teetered and fell. He didn't fall down. He just dangled there. He'd made a final effort and grabbed the ladder, and he was stuck on the end of it, too light to pull it down. I grabbed his legs and heaved, and half a minute later we'd got it down, and he was up it, and I was following.

The moment I was up there, I started pulling the ladder back in place. I could hear them talking out in the yard now. They were talking loudly, excitedly. It was a heavy old ladder, solid wood, and I didn't think I was going to manage it in time. I was sick with fright. I could feel the sickness rising in my throat. I pulled and heaved, and Soldier did, too, and the last bit of ladder came up suddenly, and caught him in the stomach, and he doubled up and went over, and *was* sick, quite quietly, in a corner.

There wasn't any time to help him. I sweated getting the ladder back exactly the way it was, and heard him, like a cat with something stuck in its throat, while I did it. He was still doing it when I finished, and I scrambled over and shoved a handkerchief in his hand, and he crammed it in front of his mouth to muffle himself. He had to, because they were there now, right outside the barn, and a man's voice was saying loudly we weren't there, we couldn't be, because there was only one set of footprints – his own.

"All the same, we look," another voice said, with a foreign accent. "They learn cunning, these boys," and then they were inside and immediately below us; about eight feet below where Soldier was being quietly sick in my handkerchief.

"Look. You're wasting time. They're not here, and they're certainly not up in the loft."

"How are you so sure?"

"Because the ladder's up there!" the farmer yelled in exasperation. "You can see it's there! I shove it there so the children can't get at it. Come on now, or you'll lose them. They're probably getting at the tractor!"

He thought of a few other things we could be getting at while the men poked about below. They didn't take any notice of him. They just went on poking. I was petrified they'd come poking up in the loft, but they took him at his word in the end and left, and I listened to their voices getting fainter, and slowly let my breath out.

It was clear enough now why the village idiot had shot back into his house, and why the farmer had locked us in. The Hungarians must have worked out where we'd jumped off the train and had been round the district warning people that a couple of Borstal boys were on the loose. That meant we had to stay away from people. It also meant we daren't risk getting a taxi. There were problems ahead – too many problems to think about at the moment. All I could think about at the moment was that we were free. While we were free there was hope.

I said, "You all right, Soldier?"

"I think so."

"Sorry about it."

"You couldn't help it."

He was still in a pretty ghastly condition and I was glad I couldn't see him. It was dark up there, the only light coming in through the trapdoor.

We crouched silently, listening.

We heard the men go in the tractor shed, and out of it, and into a barn, and out of that, too. Then the farmer got some bee in his bonnet that we'd sneaked back into the house, and he went in to see. But not all of them went in with him, which was just as well, because it gave us our only bit of luck of the day. There was a shout suddenly, and the car started up, and people came running from the house, yelling.

"Look – over there! That's them! By the wood – two boys running with a sledge!"

And in a couple of minutes they'd taken off, by car and foot, to where we were supposed to be running with a sledge into the wood, and Soldier and I settled back a bit more comfortably.

"What do we do now?" Soldier whispered.

"Wait till it's dark."

It got dark about two o'clock in the loft, but we stayed where we were because we knew it wouldn't be dark out-side yet. We thought we'd better give it till four.

They had the wireless on loud in the house, and we kept track of the time by that. We heard Forces' Favourites and carol singing and a kids' party going on in a hospital some-where. Then they did the round-the-world hook-up they do every Christmas, and we heard what everybody round the world had for their Christmas dinner. They had turkey and goose and plum pudding. We had mince pies for ours. They'd got a bit mashed in Soldier's pocket, but we ate them and had a look to see if there was anything else to eat, carrots or turnips or anything, but there wasn't. So we sat and heard what they had round the world.

A gale of wind blew up through the trapdoor and we huddled as far from it as we could, half frozen and ravenously hungry.

We didn't talk much. There wasn't much to talk about. We knew we had to keep away from people – which meant no lifts and no taxis – and that we had about seven miles to cover to Little Gippings. We'd have to cover them on foot, in the dark. With the snow, and my leg, we couldn't do more than a mile and a half an hour. So if we got out of the loft at four we ought to get there by nine.

It wasn't much of a prospect. We sat and thought about it, in the icy blast from the trapdoor, and waited for the pips on the wireless to tell us when it was four and time to go.

A bit of traffic passed on the main road while we waited, and once during the afternoon someone came out of the house and shovelled coal. That was about all that happened.

I tried to sleep, huddled up with my arms round my legs and my chin on my knees, and I must have succeeded, because the next thing I knew, Soldier was shaking me, and it was time.

Chapter Seventeen

———◆———

I WAS STIFF as a board and numb all over. The wind was moaning through the trapdoor, and it certainly hadn't got any warmer. We took a bit of time to rub the feeling back into our hands and legs, and then shuffled about in the pitch blackness looking for the ladder.

It seemed to have got about ten feet longer, enormously heavy and unmanageable in our frozen and exhausted state, and at first we couldn't budge it at all. It seemed to be nailed to the floor there. It wasn't till he started snivelling that I realized why. We'd been working side by side without any leverage.

I said, "All right, wrap up. Leave it for a minute," and did what you're supposed to do at moments of crisis – worked it out. Then I shoved him on the trapdoor end, and took the other myself, and we got out the way we came in, with him dangling on the end and using his weight, and me directing.

It's wonderful what a bit of success can do. We weren't any warmer, and we weren't any fuller, but we suddenly seemed a lot more in charge. It wasn't so ghastly down there, either. There were lights on in the house now, and we could see them. There were lights on in the drive, too, little red fairy lights for Christmas. So we took a minute or two in the barn and worked out the next step.

Since it was dark, I thought we could chance the drive. There was no point tiring ourselves out right away by going across the field in the deep snow. The drive was the quickest way to the road, and the only snag was you had to go round the house to get to it.

We watched the house for a bit. As we watched someone went round drawing curtains.

I said, "What do you think?"

"Whatever you say," Soldier said.

We watched a bit longer.

I said, "All right," and drew a deep breath. "Here goes."

We stepped out of the barn.

It was cold, blustery and much darker now the curtains were drawn. We went cautiously round the house, ready to drop flat if anything happened. Nothing did. We crunched softly round it and into the drive.

The little red fairy lights were swaying in the wind both sides of the drive. They didn't give much light, but if anyone happened to look from the house they might see our dark shapes. So we stuck to the cover of the trees. The trees were bare and didn't offer much cover, but we kept to opposite sides and moved briskly.

The lights were swaying and winking all the way to the gate, and there was one over the gate, too. There must have been a stronger breeze there, because it was winking more than the others. As we got close it suddenly struck me it was winking a *lot* more than the others. Winking too brightly. Winking much too brightly.

I stopped dead, and Soldier stopped dead, too, and in the same moment red sparks blew off the light, and I caught a whiff of it.

It wasn't a fairy light. It was a cigar, and a familiar figure was smoking it, leaning on the gate with his silk scarf and his coat collar turned up, watching us. He'd watched us all the way down the drive, and he must have been smiling all the way, as he was smiling now.

I seemed to take root then, shock draining every bit of energy out of me. But Soldier didn't. I heard a sort of squeak and a gasp and he scuttled out from the cover of the trees and started running back up the drive. He ran in a panic, sliding and slipping about on the freezing snow and whimpering like a dog. He didn't seem to know where he was running, and there wasn't much point in him running anyway, because two men were walking towards him. They were walking from the way we'd just come, and it was obvious they'd been watching us, too.

He let out a squeal just as they got their hands on him, an unearthly shriek that made my blood freeze, and then he was down on the ground, kicking and throwing himself about and trying to wriggle between their legs. He was shouting "Help!" and "Police!" and "Murderers!" and anything else he could think of. And then the gate opened and the man with the cigar came towards me, and I started yelling, too. I just yelled "Help!" But I yelled it quite a bit. It's catching when somebody starts yelling.

Like all the other times when a lot happened, I'm not too clear what went on then. I remember the noise bothered them more than anything, and they tried to muffle us, and we bit them and kicked out, and then lights were flashing from the house, and the farmer came running out, and his wife with him.

He didn't know the men had been hanging about round his house, and he was confused at all the row. A heck of a row was going on. We'd just been yelling anything we could think of, but Soldier started yelling something different then. He yelled, "Please, sir, don't believe them! They're criminals!" and I took it up.

I yelled, "Ring Dr Nixon! Ring him at Little Gippings! He'll tell you the truth! Don't let them take us!" But I doubt if they heard me. They were frog-marching us now, down the drive, to the gate, to where they had the car parked well off the track. And the boss of the school was giving his own version. He was apologizing for having his men on the farmer's land. He was saying you had to be very careful with boys like us, we were tricky and dangerous. He'd had an idea we hadn't left the property and would try to break out when it was dark. He hadn't wanted to alarm anybody in case we managed to escape in the confusion. So he'd let us come out by ourselves, and get in the drive, so he could block it both ends, and we wouldn't have a chance.

He was coming out with all this pretty loudly, to drown our voices, and he was succeeding, because we were being marched briskly ahead, and he was following on more slowly with the farmer and his wife.

I could hear she wasn't happy about it. She kept saying we were only young boys, and we couldn't have done anything very serious, and she hoped we wouldn't be punished for running away.

I thought if I could speak to her directly I might have a chance – put some doubts in her mind, anyway. But there wasn't much hope of that. They started bundling us in the car before the party got level, and once we were in they slammed the doors shut fast. But the boss of the school had to get in, too, and just as he opened the door, I broke loose of the man holding me, and leaned over the seat-back, and got a brief glimpse of the woman, and yelled at her as loudly and clearly as I could.

I'd thought about it, and I knew I had to get the words right in the shortest possible time. I yelled, "My name's *Woolcott*! Ring *Nixon*, at Little Gippings. It's *Doctor* Nixon. Tell him – " And that was all I said, because a rolled-up scarf went in my mouth, went in hard, and right in, so that I started choking on it. And the front door slammed, and we were away, and that was the last chance gone.

The chap who'd rammed the scarf in was feeling spiteful, and he still didn't take it out even though there was no point in gagging me now. He rammed it in harder, practically down my throat, and screwed it round, bruising me with his knuckles. But grim as it was, I was conscious of something a lot grimmer.

A ghastly, hollow, hopeless feeling in the pit of my stomach told me we'd really had it now.

Chapter Eighteen

◆

THEY PUT THE blindfolds on after about half an hour. It wasn't a very pleasant half-hour. I suppose they'd not had such a marvellous time of it themselves, chasing after us, and hanging about in the cold, and then getting kicked and bitten. Anyway, they worked off a bit of their irritation on us. The bloke started clouting me about the head and ears even before he got the gag out, and Soldier's bloke did the same for him.

Soldier was crying, but he wasn't frightened now. He always seemed to find an extra bit of courage at the last moment, and I marvelled at it again, even through my own clouting. He just kept yelling, through his sobs and tears, and wouldn't stop even when the bloke bashed him. And the funny thing was they stopped bashing him first. He seemed to embarrass them. But it didn't stop Soldier. Every now and again he'd think of something else and say it. He said his father's name a couple of times, Professor Szolda, and what sounded like 'Academy'. I suppose he was telling them what a shower they were, and I cringed in my seat and prayed he'd dry up, because whatever they were going to do to us I hoped they'd do quickly without working off a lot of old scores, and he was giving them a few to work off.

They put the blindfolds on before we got to the first lights. It looked like a biggish village, but we never had the chance to see because the leader turned in his seat and muttered something and they tied the handkerchieves round our heads.

I hadn't a clue which way we were going, except it wasn't to King's Lynn. The car had turned in the wrong direction for that. I tried to work out where we could be going.

I remember in a book once some kid was captured and tied in a sack and flung in the back of a car. And this young genius remembered every turn they took, *fifteen* different turns, and worked out where they were going, and wrote himself a note, all inside the sack, and made a hole in it, and managed to chuck it out when someone opened the car door. And some way, I can't remember which, the police found the note and caught the crooks and they gave this kid a medal. I reckon he earned it.

I managed the first three changes of direction, got a bit hazy on the fourth, and a bit fed up on the fifth. After that I fell asleep. It was hot in the car and my mind had started going back over all that had happened ...

And then I wasn't asleep, and my head was being pushed down behind the seat-back and the scarf was in my mouth again.

The car was pulling into a garage for petrol.

I listened intently to see if I could tell anything from the garage man's accent. But he didn't say anything, only "Righto", and "Ta". And then we were away again, and that was that.

I couldn't hear anything out of Soldier.

I said, "Soldier?"

He said, "Yes." He wasn't next to me. There was a man next to me, and then Soldier, and then another man.

I said, "You all right?"

"Yes."

"Keep quiet," the leader growled from the front, and the bloke next to me gave my wrists a quick twist. He'd got both wrists in his hand, so I shouldn't get at the blindfold.

I kept quiet. I didn't want to say any more to Soldier. I only wanted to know he was there and okay. He seemed okay.

I felt brighter after the sleep. We seemed to be in a bit of traffic and going slower now. There wasn't any snow on the road, just wetness; you could hear the tyres hissing. I thought we must be on the outskirts of a town; and just a bit later knew I was right when we began pulling up at traffic lights and heavier traffic built up round us.

There was a bus crawling on our left, and a couple of scooters on our right, keeping pace, so I knew we must be in a traffic jam. And nearer into the centre the street filled up with people, hundreds of them, crossing at zebras and chattering and laughing – going off to Christmas parties, probably. It was still the same old day, the same old ghastly Christmas Day.

It seemed to me presently I must be going mad – letting myself be carried slowly past all these people, thousands of people, without even an effort to save myself.

I thought: I've got to stop this, and worked out a lot of ways how I could do it. I thought I could snatch the blindfold off and jump up and shove my head out of the window and start yelling. Except the window wasn't open. Or I could hammer on it, bang on the glass and shout and make signs. Except whoever noticed would probably think it a joke.

They probably thought it was a joke now – a couple of boys wearing blindfolds in the back of a car. Or maybe they put it down to eye trouble. Or maybe they didn't even notice at all. Why should they notice? We weren't causing any bother. I tried to think of some ways we might cause bother.

The only way I could think of was to grab the wheel and steer into a scooter. That would cause bother all right. Except I knew I'd be right back in my seat with my ear belted off long before I could get at the wheel.

So in the end I didn't do anything, just sat there feeling sick and low, listening to all the activity of a busy town, as we went through it at a walking pace. The only consolation was that Soldier didn't do anything either. I knew he'd have thought of a few things. And I knew the thought of a belting wouldn't bother him, if he thought it would do any good.

There comes a point after you've run enough, and failed enough, when you don't care any more. I suppose we'd both reached it then. The car came out of town and hit the open road. The engine picked up speed again, the tyres started to hiss.

I went to sleep.

We were stopped each time I woke. The first time we were in a town, in traffic, engines and voices all around. I licked my lips. I said, "Soldier?"

He didn't answer.

I went to sleep again.

Next time, it was quiet. I woke up and heard the engine

ticking softly, windscreen wipers going. The men were talking quietly. They were looking up a map. It was smoky in the car, cigar smoke.

I said, "Can we have a window open?"

"It is open," Soldier said.

"What time is it?"

"Keep quiet," a man said.

The car started reversing. It reversed a long way. I went to sleep listening to it.

And then it was quiet again, too quiet, and I came awake terrified, out of a nightmare. There was no sound at all, no engine, no wipers.

A door opened. A man's voice said softly, "Still asleep?"

"Yes."

"Don't wake them up. Carry them in."

I pretended I was asleep. I was confused, too scared to think straight. The door opened my side and I was eased out, and someone had my shoulders and someone else my legs.

There was a breeze blowing, a fresh breeze, and I was carried first on hard ground, then what seemed like pebbles, shingle. I had an idea we were near the sea.

A bit of commotion broke out behind, an exclamation and a scuffle – evidently Soldier waking up. The leader said something sharply, and Soldier's voice went muffled. But he must have been struggling because the footsteps behind started to stagger unevenly over the shingle.

Then we were off the shingle, on to soft ground; and then hard, paving-stones or concrete. We were in a doorway, and going through it – and one of the clots managed to bang my head, quite hard, against the doorpost, and I thought I'd better wake up.

"He's waking up," the clot said.

"All right. Put him down now ... You're all right," the leader's voice said to me.

I felt myself lurching a bit, not sure of my feet. A hand held me.

I said, "Where am I?"

"Never mind. You'll be in bed soon."

I put a hand up to the blindfold, but someone whipped it down again quick. Soldier was brought in behind me. Then we were both on our own pins.

"This way," the leader said.

There was a familiar sort of smell. I couldn't quite place the smell. I wondered if Soldier could place it. Someone was steering me from behind, and something was going on in front, something heavy being dragged. I tripped. A roll of carpet. A hand steadied me.

"We are going down steps," the leader's voice said. "Give me your hand."

Wooden steps, rickety steps. A damp mouldy smell came up. We got to the bottom. Soldier followed me down.

"Over here now."

We walked a few paces and stopped.

"All right. Now we can take this off."

Hands came up and untied the blindfold. I blinked in the light. There wasn't a tremendous lot of light, two bulbs about forty watts each, but bright after the blindfold. We were in a cellar and the two men with us had to bend, the roof was so low. There were a couple of mattresses on the floor, and bedding. One of the men was the leader, and he looked a bit washed-out now. There was an old wooden chair there, and he sat on it, rubbing his eyes.

He said, "Well, you'd better get to sleep. I don't think you'll be cold, there's lots of blankets."

Nobody said anything, but in the silence Soldier's tummy suddenly rumbled.

The man looked at us a moment. He said, "I forgot, you'll be hungry. I suppose you'd better have something to eat," but the way he said it, a bit sad, and as if he was thinking of something else, it didn't seem there was any point in us having anything to eat.

He blew out his breath and rubbed his eyes a bit more, and stood up.

"I'll see about it," he said. "You can get undressed, anyway."

They went, but we didn't get undressed. We just looked at each other. There was a deathly damp chill in there, and I couldn't stop trembling. My teeth were rattling. I noticed suddenly Soldier wasn't looking at me, but through me, as if I wasn't there. I'd seen him looking horrible before, but he was looking worse now. He was shaking all over, his whole body writhing as if he was having a quiet convulsion. Then he sort of folded up on his mattress, and sat there looking in my direction but without seeing me. And after a minute I got down on the other mattress. We didn't say anything. We just sat there, turned towards each other.

I'd never been so frightened in my life. I was in a paralytic fright. I couldn't seem to do anything. I didn't seem able to control my limbs. I couldn't even bother looking round the cellar. There wasn't much to look round, anyway. It was long and narrow, of grim grey brick, and there was nothing in it apart from the mattresses and the chair and the two bare light bulbs. The steps came down from a trapdoor, and they'd shut it again when they went up.

All I could think of was the tone of the man's voice. It hadn't been a niggly tone. I wished it had been niggly. It had just been – sorry. As if he'd worked out what he had to do, and there was nothing else he *could* do, and he was sorry about it.

I wondered how they'd do it.

The trapdoor went suddenly, and my heart gave a single sickening lurch. But it wasn't anyone coming down to do anything. It was just the chap with the food. I'd forgotten about the food. He still had his coat and scarf on, and he was by himself. He had a tray with two mugs of cocoa and a plate of wrapped biscuits. He seemed a bit upset we were just sitting there.

He said, "Oh, look, you'll be cold. There's no reason why you should be cold. Get into bed. Wrap yourselves up well ... I'm afraid there's only biscuits. They're chocolate digestive biscuits. I hope you like chocolate digestive biscuits."

He seemed to be talking just to break the silence, because nobody else said anything. Soldier and I just stared at him as if he was a snake or something.

He put the tray on the floor and gave me a mug and said, "Here, drink it."

I took it, but I didn't drink it. I thought he might have put something in it. He gave Soldier the other mug, but Soldier didn't even take it. He just stared at him, and presently the man put it down. He said to me, "Drink it while it's hot."

I put the mug up to my lips, but I didn't drink. I just

pretended to drink. He sat down and watched me. He didn't seem to want to go.

He said, "How old are you?"

"Fourteen."

He said, "Fourteen. Yes. I have a boy in Hungary who will now be fourteen. I hope he will be as brave and resourceful as you. You are a good boy – both of you – very good boys."

He took out his handkerchief and blew his nose, and stood up and walked up and down a bit, with his head bent because of the low roof. He blew his nose quite a bit more. When he came back, I saw his eyes were red. It suddenly struck me, incredibly, he'd been crying.

He sat down and leaned forward and rumpled my hair. He said, "You know, do not always believe the worst in people. With human beings there is no such thing as black and white – just varying shades of grey. The most they can achieve is a lighter shade of grey. Do you understand that?"

I said, "No."

"No. You're very young. Fourteen," he said, and gave a watery smile.

I wondered, if he thought I was such a good kid, if he was going to let me be fifteen ever. I cleared my throat. I said cautiously, "What are you going to do with us?"

He didn't say anything for a minute. He just looked at me, smiling a bit sombrely. And when he did, he was back on his black-white-grey kick.

He said, "People try to be white. They try to do only what is right. But they can't. In the end, most often, they have to choose only what seems the least wrong ... Do you know what blackmail is?"

I said, "Yes." I had a sort of idea.

He said, "This man Kallai, the cripple, was blackmailing me. He was blackmailing all of us, eight of us. And yet it was not for his own good. He was only trying to achieve a lighter shade of grey ... "

And suddenly he started talking about it, very quickly, and not always in English, so I only got to the bottom of it when Soldier told me the missing bits during the night.

It seemed the cripple had a son in Hungary who was mixed up some way with the secret service there. And they were going to kick him out or do away with him because he'd failed somehow. And to save himself he'd dreamed up some idea of getting a network of spies going in England. And if it came off, he'd be okay. So what he'd done, he'd got in touch with his dad, the cripple, and given him the names of people who'd run away during the revolution, people who still had relations in Hungary. And the cripple had to blackmail these people – he had to get them to work as spies. And if they wouldn't he said their relations in Hungary would cop it.

That was about all the story, because we knew the rest of it – most of it, anyway. What we didn't know was how our intervention had changed their plans. They planned to knock off the cripple and then get out of the country, all of them, for a year or two until everyone had forgotten Kallai's disappearance, and then come back again. They reckoned that if they knocked him off secretly enough, the secret service in Hungary couldn't be sure that the British authorities hadn't found out about him and just disposed of him themselves. And that way, their relations wouldn't suffer.

But once we knew about it, everything was altered. They couldn't just let us go free with the information we had, because they knew at some time we'd manage to convince somebody. So they had to do three things – pretty quickly.

They had to cancel the immediate arrangements they'd made to leave the country. They had to get us. And they had to keep the cripple alive. Because he wasn't dead. That was the biggest surprise of the lot. He was pretty badly injured, but he wasn't dead. One of them was a surgeon, and he'd managed to keep him alive. They had to keep him alive, because if the plan didn't come off they didn't want a murder on their plate.

But now they'd got us, and the plan could come off – and they had three other things to do very quickly. They had to make fresh arrangements to leave the country. They had to dispose of the cripple. And they had to attend to us.

I didn't have to ask what he meant by the last. He'd get excited while he was telling the story, but he wasn't excited then. He was just sad, miserable, very quiet.

He kept asking if I understood, if I agreed, and he explained it so reasonably, so simply, that in the end I actually said yes.

He stood up then. He was pretty dead-beat. He said, "Well, I'll leave you now. Try and get some sleep."

I said, "When will you be – going?" because he'd said we would be 'attended to' just before they did go.

"I'm not sure. Tomorrow, anyway. In the afternoon, probably. Forget about that."

And then he went, and Soldier and I looked after him. There was a sound of scuffling, and then of something being dragged, after he'd shut the trapdoor – the same sounds I heard when we came in the place. I thought I knew what they were now. The scuffling was carpet being laid in place. I remembered tripping over a roll. The dragging was a heavy piece of furniture going over it.

They weren't taking any chances now.

We didn't get a lot of sleep that night. I don't think Soldier slept at all. At first, he wouldn't eat anything, either. I couldn't see the point of that. I thought if they were going to knock us off it might as well be this way as any other, but I didn't think it would be this way. And in the end he couldn't stand the sight of me eating, and said he'd nibble a bit just to see. He managed to nibble through all his three biscuits. He even nibbled the crumbs left in the silver paper.

He got up and had a look round the place after that. I got in bed. I couldn't see anything much was going to happen to us tonight, and it was cold and damp in the cellar.

He said, "There's a watermark on these bricks. It's been flooded some time."

I got up and had a look with him. The watermark came to within a few inches of the ceiling. I didn't say anything to him but I went looking round on my own. I was looking for a grid or a steel door. I had a pretty good idea how the place had come to be flooded. I remembered the idea I had we were somewhere near the sea. I wondered if the cellar jutted out under the sea, if all you had to do to let the sea in was to open a grid or a steel door …

I couldn't see anything like that, just grey rough brick.

But the brick could be false. I didn't see how it could be opened. But there was an answer to that, too. The controls could be somewhere upstairs, out of the cellar. The light switch was out of the cellar; I couldn't see it inside, anyway, and the lights were still on.

I thought if the sea came in and covered the light sockets there'd be a short circuit. It could fuse the house. It could fuse near-by buildings, too. So if they wanted to flood the place, they'd probably turn off the current first. The only warning we'd get would be that the lights would go off …

I wondered if they *would* want to flood the place; if that was the way they'd be choosing … There were any number of ways. I got back in bed, and lay there in a state of sick calm while I went through them. They could wait till we were asleep and come down and shoot us. Or a sudden blow with a hammer. A thrust with a knife. Chloroform. A drug injection. Poison. Gas … A little gas cylinder, dropped through the trapdoor and quietly leaking away while we slept … And then, after the right amount of time had elapsed, the sea door opening and water flooding in to wash out the gas, and us with it …

There were so many ways that in the end they didn't seem horrific, just crazy and weird, nothing to do with me. You can't imagine such a thing happening. You can't imagine yourself dying. And anyway, he'd said we probably wouldn't be till the afternoon. Of course, that could have been a lie, too. There wasn't anything I could do about it, either way.

I said, "Get to sleep, Soldier."

He said, "All right."

He got down in his blankets, but he didn't get to sleep. His eyes stayed open, on the lights. I wondered if he'd worked out about the lights, and what it meant if they went off. I didn't say anything in case he hadn't. But I thought of something else then.

I said, "Did you smell anything when we came in?"

He said, "Smell what?"

"I don't know. A funny sort of smell. I've smelt it before."

He said, "What *kind* of smell?"

"I don't know what kind. I wouldn't ask you if I knew. Either you smelt it or you didn't."

"I didn't," Soldier said.

I said, "All right. Get to sleep," and turned over to see if I could get some.

I did, after a bit.

He was still awake when I woke. He was looking at the lights.

I said, "Why don't you sleep?"

"I can't," Soldier said.

"Shut your eyes."

"I don't want to."

"Why not?"

"I don't want to," Soldier said.

I sat up. He looked like a ghost. He had the blankets up to his chin and his face was white and trembling. All of him was trembling under the blankets.

I said, "Look, you won't do yourself any good staying awake."

"I know," he said.

"They won't do anything tonight."

"They might."

"He said they wouldn't."

"They *might*," he said. "You know they might!" It was hard to make out *what* he said, his mouth was trembling so much. He was looking at me like a dog that's hurt and wants you to do something for it. There wasn't anything I could do.

I just said, "Soldier, even if they do, what can we do about it?"

"Nothing!" he said. He seemed to bawl it out, because he hadn't got any control of his voice.

I said quietly, "So why not go to sleep?"

"Because I want to know about it," he said.

"It won't do you any good."

"I still want to know."

I didn't want to, so I turned over and tried to get to sleep again. I couldn't get to sleep. I lay pretty still and breathed quietly so he should think I was.

After a bit he started crying.

It was more of a hum than a cry. I thought at first he'd started singing. My hair stood on end. I thought he'd gone out of his mind and started singing. But he was crying, lying there crying in terror. It struck me he might have been doing it earlier before I woke up.

I sat up. He tried to stop it when he saw me. He managed to get his mouth shut, anyway. It still kept coming, through his nose. It was a low, bubbling, hysterical moan.

I didn't say anything. I just got up and shifted my mattress next to his and pulled the blankets over both of us, and put my arm round him. He piped down after that.

He was icy cold and his limbs kept jerking. And his teeth rattled and he had a fit of trembling every now and then.

But it seemed to help, having me next to him. We got through the night like that, anyway.

We had Smiler in the morning. We heard the trapdoor going and sat up and he came down the steps with a tray. There were two glasses of milk on the tray, and a plate of bread and butter. They'd only had biscuits last night, so I thought they must have got the bread this morning. I wondered what time it was.

I said, "What time is it?"

He put the tray down and went.

He wasn't one of the more lovable ones, Smiler. Just at the top of the steps he turned and grinned at us. It was more of a snarl than a grin, and I remembered something Soldier said during the night. He said Smiler had wanted to knock us off right away, it made him nervous having us around. Only the leader had stopped him. He'd said nobody was getting knocked off till they were certain they were going. So we had that to thank him for anyway.

I got up and tried to eat some of the bread and butter, but I was all of a twitch and I couldn't. It stuck in my throat. I didn't get back on the mattress after that. I just walked up and down the cellar. I couldn't keep still. I thought they must have had a lot of things to do this morning, and seeing to our breakfast wouldn't be the most important of them. So it was probably pretty late now, after ten, maybe after eleven. In the afternoon, he'd said, they'd be going ...

I couldn't hear anything up above. We hadn't heard anything all night, the roof was so solid. I wondered if I dared go up and listen at the trapdoor. The danger was Smiler might be there, and he'd welcome the excuse ... I looked back at Soldier, but he wasn't looking at me. He was just looking at the wall, sitting huddled in his blankets.

I went cautiously up the steps and put my ear to the trapdoor. I still couldn't hear anything. So I got my hands up and tried to shift it. It went up a fraction of an inch and then wouldn't go any more. There was carpet there, holding it down, and something very solid on the carpet. But I could hear something now, faint vibrations, muffled footsteps.

The footsteps didn't seem too far away. They seemed to be getting nearer. I suddenly realized they were very near, on top of me, and the furniture was being shifted and the carpet moving.

I let go of the trapdoor and practically fell down the steps, shaking like a jelly. I thought this was it, the moment had come. I was over in the far corner when he came down the steps. I was leaning up against the angle of the wall, and my legs were shaking so much I couldn't stand. I felt myself slipping slowly down till I was half squatting there. And he came over, quite slowly, smiling a bit in a sad, concerned sort of way.

He said, "Please don't be frightened. Don't be. We aren't going yet."

It was the leader, and he'd changed now. He had an old pair of trousers on and a navy-blue jersey like a seaman. He had his sleeves rolled up and he was dusty as if he'd been carrying old trunks and luggage.

I couldn't speak. I just looked up at him and my eyes seemed to glaze over with panic so that he had two heads.

He said, "I don't want you to be frightened. There's no need – I promise."

I heard myself talking then. I didn't even know I was talking.

I said, "When are you going?"

He said, "In just over an hour. At one o'clock."

"Will you let us know – when it's time?"

"You'll know," he said. "Just forget about it … I came across this. I thought you might like it."

He had a little book in his hand and he gave me it and I took it.

He said, "I'll see you again," and went.

I was so petrified I couldn't see what book it was. I just kept looking down at it, after the trapdoor shut. It took about a couple of minutes to see it was a Bible.

I got up then. I blundered over to the mattress and sat down. Soldier wasn't sitting up in his blankets now. He was lying flat, staring at the ceiling.

I said, "I've got a Bible here, Soldier." I said it in a sort of astonishment and my voice came out squeaky and uneven.

After a bit he said, "Read it. Read it out."

I opened it, and it came open at Psalms. It came open at Psalm 23. I said, "Psalm twenty-three," and started saying it. I said:

" 'The Lord is my shepherd: I shall not want,' " and went on right the way through to:

" 'Yea, though I walk through the valley of the shadow of death, I will fear no evil: for thou art with me: thy rod and thy staff they comfort me.' "

I stopped then, because he was saying it. He was saying it

in Hungarian. He said it all, and then he said, "Read some more," and I turned the page and found I couldn't. The words had started blurring. I suddenly realized I was crying. I hadn't meant to cry. I hadn't cried for years. But I was doing it then, all over the page, and I felt such a nit I dropped the book. He just sat up and took it, and went on himself. I don't know what he read. I didn't even listen. But in some peculiar way the sound of the words made me feel better. It knocked me off snivelling, anyway.

Then he shut the book and lay back, and I lay back with him. I looked up at the ceiling for a bit, but after a while I didn't even do that. I closed my eyes and felt myself wandering about in darkness. I felt I was in a dark valley, in the valley of the shadow of death, like it said, and it was a pretty accurate description, and I didn't care any more. The only thing I cared about, I was sorry I was so far from home, stuck away on a rotten cold bit of coast, and my mother wouldn't know about it. But I didn't want to think of my mother. I tried not to think about her.

I lay on the mattress, and knew I wouldn't be getting off it. They could come and do it there, and all I hoped was that they'd do it quickly.

I lay there, aware of my body for the last time; feet and legs, hands and arms, eyes and ears; all the things that were me, and that wouldn't be for much longer.

After a bit I felt so remote they hardly seemed to be mine at all. I knew nothing was ever going to frighten me again. I wouldn't be afraid when the trapdoor opened. I wouldn't be afraid when the man came down, all alone, on his last job. And then the trapdoor did open, and it was true I wasn't afraid. I didn't even feel a tremor. I just lay there, feeling very weary, feeling very heavy, about a ton, and I couldn't even bother opening my eyes.

I heard him say quietly, "Are you there?" and start coming down, and I still didn't open them.

Then he said it again, and I did. Because it wasn't the man I'd been expecting, and he wasn't alone. It was Dr Nixon. And he had eight policemen and two dogs with him.

We were asleep soon after that. We had an injection each, Soldier and me, and were carried up the steps and out of the trapdoor. I was unconscious before we got to the cars, but I wasn't when we came out of the house and saw where we were. There wasn't any shingle and there wasn't any sea. There was just a gravel drive – the pebbles I'd heard crunching when we were carried in – and the house was the one in Amberley Park.

I'd imagined myself dying far from home, and all the time we hadn't been ten minutes away. For some reason it suddenly struck me as funny, very funny indeed, and I heard myself starting to laugh. I was still laughing when I lost consciousness.

Chapter Nineteen

HE SAID, "Hello. Welcome back."

I said, "Thanks," and tried to sit up.

"Are you hungry?"

I said, "Yeah. Pretty."

"For soup or something more solid?"

I said, "Something more solid," and he smiled and said, "I thought so. It's coming up."

It was Dr Nixon, and I seemed to have been seeing a lot of him. I seemed to have been seeing a lot of soup, too. I'd keep waking up and there'd be a bowl of soup, with Dr Nixon or my mother behind it. All the way through the soup I'd try to sort out the questions in my mind. There were so many I couldn't get them sorted out. I didn't even know where to begin, or how to put them into words. Just at the end of the bowl I'd think of a useful question like, "Where am I?" and open my mouth to ask it, and someone would pop a capsule in and say, "Swallow that," and I'd swallow it and go to sleep again immediately.

I'd been doing it a long time. But things had got clearer. They were clearer each time I woke. I knew I was home now, in my own room. I knew Soldier was home in his.

I said, "What day is it?"

"Wednesday."

Wednesday. I worked it out and said cautiously, "You mean – three days after Christmas?"

He said, "That's right. That's very good. Very good indeed," and he said it again, for my mother's benefit, because she was coming in with a tray.

She said, "Hello. What do you say to a couple of poached eggs on toast?"

I said, "Wow!"

"He's all right now," Dr Nixon said, standing up. "I'll run along and see the other one. Don't tell him till he's eaten."

"Don't tell me what?" I said when she got back from seeing him out.

"Anything," she said. "You just get on with it."

I'd got on with it. I was practically through it. I felt ravenous. I felt marvellous. I'd never felt so marvellous in my life. I'd expected to be dead, and I was alive. I wanted to do everything, and eat everything, and jump about and sing at the same time. I couldn't get through it quick enough. I forked in the last mouthful and gave her the plate.

She said, "All right, don't choke yourself. There's apple pie and ice-cream yet," and then, "Well, well. What's that for?"

"Just for fun," I said, and gave her another, and she tried not to look pleased, and couldn't, because we don't go in for kissing much, normally.

She said, "Well, well," again, and then, "We'll have to lock you up in a cellar every day, won't we?"

Then I polished off the apple pie and ice-cream, and she told me.

It seemed it was the woman at the farm who'd started the ball rolling, but she hadn't done it till next morning.

She'd remembered what I'd yelled at her, and she'd rung up the local police to ask after the two escaped Borstal boys. They'd said, "What escaped Borstal boys?" and then she'd told them.

Things happened pretty quickly after that. The police had telephoned Dr Nixon, and *he'd* telephoned my mother. She'd been quietly going out of her mind since Saturday lunch-time when I hadn't turned up at the shop. She'd been practically camping out at the police station to see if there was any news of us, and the only reason she wasn't there then was that it was very early in the morning. The farmer's wife had started everything going early. She hadn't slept too well, thinking about it, and she'd phoned the police at six.

After that, everything went into top gear. Dr Nixon drove down to see if he was needed. The police checked up their report book and decided to investigate the other story again. They'd wasted a bit of time looking for the bogus cripple because the house in Burlington was empty; then they'd tried to get in touch with the proprietor of the school, only he was 'away' too. So in the end they'd tried the school in Amberley Park, and had got suspicious when they realized a lot of activity was going on in it. They kept watch for a while, and meanwhile requested official permission to enter and search it.

The permission had turned up about the same time as Dr Nixon, and they went in together and rounded up the whole shower without a fight. Only Smiler had tried to run for it, and he hadn't run far. You can't with a police dog on your back. And then the leader had told the police the whole story. They hadn't meant to kill us – just gag and tie us up so they could have time to get away. And then they'd have let the police know where we were. They had some idea that by that time, once the police understood, the whole matter could be hushed up so the news wouldn't get back to Hungary, and their original intention would have worked.

We weren't the only prisoners in the house. They'd got the cripple there, too. And they *had* meant to kill him – just before they went. He was in hospital now, and in a bad way; but he wouldn't have been even that way if it wasn't for us. So something had come out of it.

I sat and thought about him for a bit. We were both pretty thoughtful when she finished the story. But my mother was thinking of something else. She said, "It beats me how any woman can act that way."

I said, "What way?"

"Letting those men take you and then waiting all night before telling anyone."

"It wasn't her fault. It sounded convincing the way they told it."

"I'll give her a piece of my mind when I see her, anyway."

"When will you see her?"

"As soon as I can. Tomorrow, probably."

"What do you mean, tomorrow?"

"When we go up there," she said.

"When we go up *where*?"

"Up to Norfolk."

"*Who's* going to Norfolk?"

"*We* are," she said. "You are, and I am, and your friend is, and his mother is," and she was smiling all over her face.

"Dr Nixon's driving us up there. He wants us to spend a holiday on the farm."

And then she was saying, "Here – you get back in bed." And then, "Well, well," and "Well, well," again, and trying not to look too pleased, and not succeeding.

The fields were still covered with snow as we went up there, only we didn't fall asleep this time. I thought of something as we drove. I said, "Here, Soldier, how was it you didn't smell that smell in there?"

He said, "What smell in where?"

"That smell in Amberley Park. I smelt it. I knew I'd smelt it before."

"I'd got a cold," he said. "I couldn't smell anything. I got it in that rotten loft."

He'd still got it. It was a well-looked-after cold now. He'd got a furry foreign overcoat on, with a great muffler round his neck, and a woolly hat with a pompom on his head. You could hardly see him in there, but what you could see was pretty chirpy. He kept pointing things out. We were going back the way we came. It wasn't the most direct way, but Dr Nixon thought we'd want to see it again.

We went up past the track across the fen that led to the shepherd's hut, and then the bus stop, and the village idiot's house, and the Donnybanks phone box, and the track up to the farm. We didn't stop there, even though my mother had a piece of her mind to unload. We went on, through Wittle, and soon after branched off, before we came to King's Lynn, and headed for Little Gippings.

There was a crossroads before you got to it, and Nixon was waiting there, jumping about to keep warm. He started jumping like mad when he saw us.

His father pulled up and said, "Now what is the point of your coming to meet us? I told you there'd be no room in the car."

"Yes, there is," Nixon said. "I can bunk in. Soldier can sit on my knee. How are you then, Soldier? Good old Soldier," he said, and kept on like that as we set off again. I gave him a bit of a look but he never even noticed. He's like that, Nixon. He can forget anything he wants to forget.

The way he went on, that day, and all the ones that followed, you'd think the three of us had always been blood-brothers, with him and Soldier special ones. Poor Soldier didn't know what to make of it, but he had no complaints, and there was no point in me getting niggly. The only time I got niggly, we were watching television, and Nixon mentioned some programme Soldier hadn't heard of, and I said quietly, "He still hasn't got a television, you know." But Nixon only blinked and changed the subject, and I was sorry I said it. He can be pretty nice, Nixon, when he wants to be, and he was trying hard then.

We went out one day to the farm near Wittle, and my mother got ready to give the woman a piece of her mind. But she never had a chance, the farmer and his wife were so apologetic. We had tea there, and the radio still played too loudly, and Soldier and Nixon and I went out and up to the loft and listened to it. And Soldier and I smiled at each other as we remembered how we'd been there before, and Nixon got a bit annoyed because he hadn't been; so we came down again.

Another day, the three of us went out to the turkey farm. We took our lunch and got the bus to the track across the fen, and walked there easily, in gumboots, not tired and desperate now, just out for fun. And we got some.

Nixon turned out to have a talent for making turkey noises, and every now and then he'd make them, and the old maniac would come rushing out with his gun, and we'd throw ourselves hysterically about in the snow, and when we had any breath told him what we thought of him. Nixon told him he was an anti-social nit, and Soldier tried to tell him he was nutty as a fruit cake. He'd heard me say it, and it tickled him, except he got it wrong and called him a teacake instead. Then we went back and had our lunch in the shepherd's hut, and caught the bus home.

But there had to be trouble with Soldier around, and he supplied it. He'd come up with a cold, and he didn't believe in keeping anything to himself. Nixon got it, and I got it, and Soldier's mother, and my mother, and Nixon's mother and his grandparents. The only one who didn't get it was Dr Nixon, and that was because he wasn't there. He'd had to go back to town to relieve his assistant, and one of the best days was when he telephoned with special news.

He had three bits of news. The first was that the cripple was on the mend and expected to pull through. The second was that the school was getting a half-holiday for what we'd done. And the third was that Soldier was going up to the Seniors. The Head had told him that. It wasn't just because of anything that had happened, of course. It was just that his work was a higher standard than they did in the Juniors, even though his English wasn't up to much. And our adventures had made the Head look into it.

"So we'll be together all the time now!" Nixon said, and I had to laugh because the way he said it you'd think he'd been praying for it all his life.

He's a funny cuss, Nixon, and so is Soldier, but that was a pretty good Christmas we had. It was the best one I ever had, really. Like a lot of other things, it hadn't started too well. It just got better all the time.

Heinemann
New Windmills

Founding Editors: Anne and Ian Serraillier

Chinua Achebe Things Fall Apart
Vivien Alcock The Cuckoo Sister; The Monster Garden;
The Trial of Anna Cotman; A Kind of Thief; Ghostly Companions
Margaret Atwood The Handmaid's Tale
Jane Austen Pride and Prejudice
J G Ballard Empire of the Sun
Nina Bawden The Witch's Daughter; A Handful of Thieves; Carrie's
War; The Robbers; Devil by the Sea; Kept in the Dark; The Finding;
Keeping Henry; Humbug; The Outside Child
Valerie Bierman No More School
Melvin Burgess An Angel for May
Ray Bradbury The Golden Apples of the Sun; The Illustrated Man
Betsy Byars The Midnight Fox; Goodbye, Chicken Little; The
Pinballs; The Not-Just-Anybody Family; The Eighteenth Emergency
Victor Canning The Runaways; Flight of the Grey Goose
Ann Coburn Welcome to the Real World
Hannah Cole Bring in the Spring
Jane Leslie Conly Racso and the Rats of NIMH
Robert Cormier We All Fall Down; Tunes for Bears to Dance to
Roald Dahl Danny, The Champion of the World; The Wonderful
Story of Henry Sugar; George's Marvellous Medicine; The BFG;
The Witches; Boy; Going Solo; Matilda
Anita Desai The Village by the Sea
Charles Dickens A Christmas Carol; Great Expectations;
Hard Times; Oliver Twist; A Charles Dickens Selection
Peter Dickinson Merlin Dreams
Berlie Doherty Granny was a Buffer Girl; Street Child
Roddy Doyle Paddy Clarke Ha Ha Ha
Gerald Durrell My Family and Other Animals
Anne Fine The Granny Project
Anne Frank The Diary of Anne Frank
Leon Garfield Six Apprentices; Six Shakespeare Stories;
Six More Shakespeare Stories
Jamila Gavin The Wheel of Surya
Adele Geras Snapshots of Paradise

Alan Gibbons Chicken
Graham Greene The Third Man and The Fallen Idol; Brighton Rock
Thomas Hardy The Withered Arm and Other Wessex Tales
L P Hartley The Go-Between
Ernest Hemmingway The Old Man and the Sea; A Farewell to Arms
Nigel Hinton Getting Free; Buddy; Buddy's Song
Anne Holm I Am David
Janni Howker Badger on the Barge; Isaac Campion; Martin Farrell
Jennifer Johnston Shadows on Our Skin
Toeckey Jones Go Well, Stay Well
Geraldine Kaye Comfort Herself; A Breath of Fresh Air
Clive King Me and My Million
Dick King-Smith The Sheep-Pig
Daniel Keyes Flowers for Algernon
Elizabeth Laird Red Sky in the Morning; Kiss the Dust
D H Lawrence The Fox and The Virgin and the Gypsy;
Selected Tales
Harper Lee To Kill a Mockingbird
Ursula Le Guin A Wizard of Earthsea
Julius Lester Basketball Game
C Day Lewis The Otterbury Incident
David Line Run for Your Life
Joan Lingard Across the Barricades; Into Exile; The Clearance;
The File on Fraulein Berg
Robin Lister The Odyssey
Penelope Lively The Ghost of Thomas Kempe
Jack London The Call of the Wild; White Fang
Bernard Mac Laverty Cal; The Best of Bernard Mac Laverty
Margaret Mahy The Haunting
Jan Mark Do You Read Me? (Eight Short Stories)
James Vance Marshall Walkabout
W Somerset Maughan The Kite and Other Stories
Ian McEwan The Daydreamer; A Child in Time
Pat Moon The Spying Game
Michael Morpurgo Waiting for Anya; My Friend Walter;
The War of Jenkins' Ear
Bill Naughton The Goalkeeper's Revenge
New Windmill A Charles Dickens Selection
New Windmill Book of Classic Short Stories
New Windmill Book of Nineteenth Century Short Stories

How many have you read?